SHARK

SHARK
A PHOTOGRAPHER'S STORY

JEREMY STAFFORD-DEITSCH

—— *FOREWORD BY* ——

PROFESSOR SAMUEL H GRUBER

SIERRA CLUB BOOKS   SAN FRANCISCO

The Sierra Club, founded in 1892 by John Muir, has devoted itself
to the study and protection of the earth's scenic and ecological
resources—mountains, wetlands, woodlands, wild shores and rivers,
deserts and plains. The publishing program of the Sierra Club offers
books to the public as a nonprofit educational service in the hope
that they may enlarge the public's understanding of the Club's basic
concerns. The point of view expressed in each book, however, does
not necessarily represent that of the Club. The Sierra Club has some
sixty chapters coast to coast, in Canada, Hawaii, and Alaska. For
information about how you may participate in its programs to
preserve wilderness and the quality of life, please address inquiries
to Sierra Club, 730 Polk Street, San Francisco, CA 94109.

Text and photographs copyright © Jeremy Stafford-Deitsch 1987
This edition copyright © Eddison/Sadd Editions 1987

Library of Congress Cataloging-in-Publication Data
Stafford-Deitsch, Jeremy.
  Shark.

  Bibliography: p.
  Includes index.
  1. Sharks.   I. Title
QL638.9.S75   1987   597'.31   87–4798
ISBN 0–87156–776–8

Jacket design by *Nick Eddison*
Book design by *Nigel Partridge*

10 9 8 7 6 5 4 3 2 1

Half title
The bulky form of a great white shark
glides beneath the surface.

Frontispiece
Lord of all it surveys, a grey reef shark
moves through the luxuriant world of a
Red Sea coral reef.

AN Eddison·Sadd edition

Edited, designed and produced by
Eddison/Sadd Editions Limited
2 Kendall Place, London W1H 3AH

Phototypeset by Bookworm Typesetting, Manchester, England
Origination by Columbia Offset, Singapore
Printing and binding in Hong Kong by Mandarin Offset

CONTENTS

FOREWORD

As a youngster, growing up in Florida around the water, I was exposed to the mystery of sharks. My real interest, however, was rekindled in college where as a pre-medical student I dissected a dogfish in comparative anatomy. But it was an encounter with a huge hammerhead while scuba-diving that turned my interest to compulsion, and I changed my life and career to study sharks. That was more than thirty years ago. Since then I have had the privilege of investigating one of the world's most magnificent and biologically sophisticated creatures. For this, I count myself among the luckiest of men. In the course of these studies, I have run across other investigators of sharks, such as Jeremy Stafford-Deitsch.

SHARK: A PHOTOGRAPHER'S STORY is a book of timely importance. With world fisheries presently expanding at an alarming rate, and fish stocks declining precipitously, relentless pressure is being placed on shark populations by commercial fishermen. The take is well over 1,000,000,000 pounds annually. For many fish stocks, this is an acceptable catch level, but for sharks it is not. Millions of years of shark evolution has produced a survival strategy very similar to that of the great whales. Their life style is characterized by very slow growth, late maturity and low reproductive capacity. For example, we found that the lemon shark requires about fifteen years to mature and reproduce; it carries its young in pregnancy for nearly a year, and reproduces only every other year. With a fifty per cent mortality rate in their first year of life, lemon sharks barely replace themselves. Fortunately, they live long lives, but if their life is cut short by over-fishing, the results can be disastrous. This is why in our lifetime, no less than five species of shark have been fished to commercial extinction. Even the plentiful North Sea dogfish stocks which supplied fish and chip shops of Britain for centuries have been fished out.

Beside the obvious commercial dislocation, what are the biological consequences of removing the top predator level of the marine ecosystem? Terrestrial examples are clear – the system is disrupted. We must now protect sharks, but because of their 'bad press' no-one cares much if they are slaughtered. The bad reputation of sharks is at odds with reality. It is true that sharks kill men and women at an annual rate of about fifty per year. However, in Florida alone, lightning kills about 300 people annually and automobiles kill 2,000. Humans kill sharks at a rate approaching 100,000,000 a year. Clearly sharks are at risk – and the wanton slaughter goes on largely in ignorance.

As noted, sharks comprise one of the oldest, most highly evolved and sophisticated groups of marine animals in existence today. The importance of Jeremy Stafford-Deitsch's book is to show the public that there is no *one* shark, but rather a variety of highly adapted species. His photography captures, as in no other book I have read or

Samuel Gruber with a juvenile tiger shark on the research ship *Cape Florida*, in Bimini, the Bahamas.

know about, the variety, power and sheer magnificence of sharks in their natural habitat. I believe it is important that the educated public becomes aware of sharks – not the myths, but the reality. Conservation alone dictates this desire, but beyond conservation, to know and appreciate the sea, the true role of the shark must be revealed. By studying this book and the unique photographs herein, the reader will surely gain insight and an appreciation of sharks and their role in the ocean.

Samuel H Gruber, Ph.D.
Professor of Biology and Living Resources
Rosenstiel School of Marine and Atmospheric Science
University of Miami
Florida

CHAPTER ONE

—AN—
INTRODUCTION

'Little we see in Nature that is ours'
WORDSWORTH

Nature has been altered. The landscapes of the planet are now mostly subjugated by man. Apart from a few scattered outposts – deserts, the polar regions, and the highest mountain ranges – there is little that we have not touched or rebuilt.

Little wonder then that the sea represents so strongly the untamed and the unknown, for it appears to be largely unaltered by man, a natural force that still has to be reckoned with. The ocean's ability to hide its wounds beneath its surface, of seeming so secure and unchanging, is its curse. For the truth is that the seas are now more threatened than threatening. Pollution, over-fishing and wanton destruction have all taken their toll.

Nevertheless, spiritual exhaustion has heightened our fascination for the sea. It is recognized as another, often hostile, world that we enter at our peril – but also as an inexhaustible source of riches to be plundered. It is populated by creatures that we interpret, all too often, in mystical terms. There are the mighty whales, benign and godlike, stone gardens of coral reef inhabited by colourful clouds of fish, and always, in the background, the feared shadow of the shark. For, in this mythical world of generalizations, 'shark' is an umbrella term that sweeps a large and diverse group of animals into a gothic focus: they are seen as evil and primitive, huge creatures that glide silently out of the depths to attack the unsuspecting swimmer in the shallows. This view has been nurtured by the media – sharks have been sensationalized into old-fashioned demons.

It is true that some species of shark occasionally attack people. While such attacks are, of course, horrific, they tend to elicit a collective hysteria that is out of all proportion to the events and which wrongly influences our conception of these animals. This is not only because of the physical injuries inflicted in an attack. It is also because we have come, through hundreds of years of increasingly secure living, to think of ourselves as somehow removed from the natural order of things: *we* are not meant to be eaten. Thus a shark attacking a human is viewed with outrage, and the shark is personalized into a loathsome creature that has broken a golden rule. The shark must be caught and destroyed. A desire for revenge and retribution seizes even the most rational among us.

This state of affairs is gradually changing. Divers often see sharks in their natural habitat and remember the experience with exhilaration. For sharks include some of the most beautiful creatures on the planet. They also include some of the most formidable predators, and

yet attacks by sharks on people are extremely rare. However tragic the attacks, these events do not justify the annihilation of sharks.

Scientific investigation of sharks continues to replace myth and cliché with fact. What popular natural history books once described as 'perfect eating-machines unchanged for hundreds of millions of years' are, in fact, highly evolved and sophisticated predators, both in terms of their structure and their behaviour. As scientists continue to study these magnificent animals, our understanding of them broadens and matures. The 'rogues of the sea that perform no useful purpose' are being recast as apex predators – animals at the top of their food chain. Their importance is seen as paramount, as they, by hunting and culling, maintain the overall fitness of the populations below them.

A diver's first view of a shark on a coral reef is usually as a powerful form moving in the background. The shark's curiosity is short-lived and it goes on its way. The diver does not forget the shark as quickly as the shark forgets the diver.

Even as recently as 1965, the great ichthyologist J.L.B. Smith, in describing the sharks of South African waters, could describe the bull shark as 'an ugly and dangerous brute' or the great white shark as 'a terror to all who venture on or in the water'. Ask a modern shark scientist (or elasmobranchologist) about sharks and you will see fear replaced by fascination. Studies of certain species of shark have revealed glimpses of intricate social patterns previously unsuspected. Furthermore, in the last few years, tremendous advances have been made in the classification of sharks. Ten years ago, sharks were a taxonomist's nightmare. The same species would turn up in various parts of the world sporting a different scientific name in each location. Different species would, because of similarities, share the same name in one location, only to be separated elsewhere. This list of problems was, inevitably, reflected in the popular literature. The more one read, the more confused one became. Now, however, the situation is considerably clearer – though not without an occasional, tremendous surprise.

In 1976, a research vessel of the United States Navy was off the Hawaiian island of Oahu. When the crew were retrieving the sea anchor, they found a large shark entangled in the cables. It appeared to have attempted to swallow the brightly coloured chute of the sea anchor. The shark was so large – 4.5 metres (15 feet) – and so odd-looking that it was not cast overboard. Rather, it was taken to the Waikiki Aquarium, where the director, Leighton Taylor, was able to study it. The flabby carcass weighed over 726 kg (1600 lb). And yet it bore little resemblance to any known species of shark. It had a huge mouth full of tiny teeth, and analysis of the stomach showed it had been feeding on small open-water shrimps. The structure of the gills revealed that it was a filter-feeder: rather than swallowing large prey whole, or biting chunks out of prey, the gills of this strange shark were modified for sieving food particles from the water. To this end, the shark's gills were equipped with filaments called gillraker papillae, which stretch across the inside of the gill slits like fine nets. The shark swims with its mouth open through the water and swallows whatever organic material becomes trapped inside the gills.   Up until then, the two largest species of shark – the whale shark *Rhincodon typus* and the basking shark *Cetorhinus maximus* – were the only known filter-feeders. Suddenly there was a third. And while its basic method of feeding was the same, it had an additional trick for capturing its prey, not seen in the whale shark or basking shark. All around its mouth were rows of tiny luminescent organs that glowed like fireflies. Many marine animals have such light organs, but they are unusual among sharks. In this species they probably serve to attract small shrimps in the plankton, luring them towards the shark's cavernous mouth.

That so large an animal could have remained undetected for such a length of time is amazing and the scientific community greeted the discovery with incredulity. Thanks to its huge mouth, the animal was nicknamed the 'megamouth shark', *Megachasma pelagios*. And it turned out to be so different from other known sharks that it was classified in its own family – Megachasmidae. Since its discovery, one more megamouth has been caught, in a gill net off Catalina Island, California, in 1984.

Even without such spectacular discoveries, sharks are fascinating animals. My own interest in them, and in all aspects of marine life, goes back to my childhood, and summer holidays on the French coast of the Mediterranean. I must have been about ten years old when I first took up snorkelling. The seascape there is comparatively dull, due to years of fishing, spear-fishing and pollution. Nevertheless, I found plenty to absorb me, and would snorkel for hours at a time.

After a few summers I needed an activity and took up spear-fishing. For several years I chased the timid and undersized fish that darted among the rocks, finally abandoning this rather primitive and pointless activity when I was thirteen or fourteen. One afternoon, after shooting yet more inedible fish, I came across a cuttlefish hovering over the bottom. Heroically, I speared it, and then watched it flash every colour in its chromatophoric armoury, as it struggled, impaled. What I had not noticed was its mate, which was nearby. The other cuttlefish glided up to its dying companion and, wrapping its tentacles around it, tried to drag it off the spear. I never used my spear again.

Scuba diving was an inevitable progression, though it took several years of begging before I was allowed to dive. The minimum age to start is considered to be fifteen, but I managed to talk the local diving club into taking me out when I was thirteen. It was about this time that I first saw Peter Gimbel's incredible film 'Blue Water, White Death'. In it, he and several other diving figures – Stan Waterman, and Ron and Valery Taylor – set off on a worldwide quest for the great white shark. They obtained superb underwater footage of oceanic whitetip sharks feeding on whale carcasses off Durban, South Africa. Eventually they travelled to South Australia where they asked Rodney Fox, himself a survivor of a great white shark attack, to bring in great whites for their cameras. As I sat entranced in the cinema, watching this remarkable film, I never dreamed that I would later meet and work with Rodney, photographing great white sharks for myself.

When I was sixteen, my grandparents invited me to the Florida Keys for a holiday. The Keys have fine coral reefs and excellent fish life. I was soon diving at every opportunity on the reefs, and making my first rather fuzzy attempts at underwater photography. I was also keeping my eyes open for sharks – but without success. By now, Peter Benchley's 'Jaws' novel had appeared and the film was in preparation. However, I was not overly caught up in the 'Jaws' mania that followed. Because I was already interested in sharks, I realized that the novel was meant to be taken with a pinch of salt. I was busy gathering my own scraps of information about sharks, often struggling to come to terms with unlikely stories and wild exaggerations. However, there were certain people to whom I listened with respect. One was Tiny Wirs, the operator and owner of the Ocean Reef Dive Shop in Florida. Tiny – 1.9 metres (6 feet 4 inches) and 113 kg (250 lb) has been diving since almost before diving was invented. He looks the part, with a massive frame, bushy beard and twinkling eyes. He has many a shark story to tell, based on years of treasure-and salvage-diving in Florida and the Bahamas. I used to quiz him endlessly about his shark adventures, and he would never tire of answering my questions. One of his best stories concerns an incident in 1963, on a wreck he was salvaging in the Bahamas. Tiny was operating an underwater suction pump: a long tube-like device

that sucks sand up off the bottom to reveal what is buried below. The instrument is difficult to hold steady, and Tiny was struggling with it as it tossed up the sand in a blinding cloud all around him. Suddenly he felt a dull ache in his right foot and he shook it. To his amazement, his foot shook back. Looking down, he could see a shark of about 1.25 metres (4 feet) in length, biting into his diving boot. A desperate struggle ensued with Tiny trying to pull the stubborn shark off his foot. Luckily the thickness of his diving boot prevented the shark from tearing his foot off. Eventually, all but exhausted, he managed to stab the shark in its belly – no easy feat as a shark's skin is extremely tough. But the animal still hung on, and now began writhing in pain. Unable to keep a grip on his knife any longer, Tiny released it, praying that the shark would abandon the struggle and swim off. To his vast relief, the fatally wounded animal (he thought it was a small mako), let go and swayed away into the distance. Tiny told me that he assumed the shark had attacked him in error: the disturbed sand had reduced the visibility, and the commotion caused by the suction pump had attracted the shark. It had attacked his foot because it mistook it for a struggling fish.

While I continued diving, in the vain hope of seeing sharks, my brother Nicholas, who had accompanied me to Florida, spent most of his days fishing. One evening he returned from a fishing trip with an expression of wild excitement on his face: he had been sitting on a rock dangling his feet in the water and wondering whether to pack up his gear and go home, when a huge grey shape passed, at high speed

Tiny Wirs photographs reef fish in the Florida Keys. He uses a Nikonos camera specially designed for underwater use. Above his right hand is a light meter and attached to the side of the camera is a flash gun to restore the natural colours that are absorbed underwater.

on the surface, right next to him. A tall thin dorsal fin cut through the surface, and then he made out a rectangular head, before the sweep of the tail carried the animal away. He recognized it as a great hammerhead, the largest and most formidable of the hammerheads. He guessed it was at least 4 metres (13 feet) long. Hammerheads are known to enter the shallow waters of the Florida Keys to feed, particularly at dusk.

By now I was getting frustrated at not having seen a shark for myself. I particularly wanted to see one underwater, so a couple of days later, along with Tiny and some other divers, I snorkelled around a shallow wreck that was impaled on dead coral inside the main reef. The water was not very clear but Tiny had suggested that it would be a good place to see a shark such as a bull shark – they like shallow water and are often attracted to wrecks, since prey animals tend to congregate round them. I grabbed my camera and was the first in, looking for sharks. I did not see any, so I snorkelled around for a while and returned to the boat. It turned out that the second person to jump into the water had landed smack on top of a startled shark – the shark had sped off in one direction, and the diver in the other. I did not seem to be having much luck.

Talking to Tiny later that day I persuaded him to take me on a special shark dive beneath a buoy called the 'whistle buoy' that was located in about 12 metres (40 feet) of water beyond the main reef. Fishermen often reported large schools of fish and good-sized sharks in this area. Nicholas came along to try to catch a shark after we had finished our dive (a conflict of interests that has persisted between me and fishermen ever since).

The next day Tiny arrived for the dive carrying a bangstick: this is an underwater weapon that can be used against sharks for defence. A bangstick (or 'powerhead' as it is also known) is a pole fitted with a chamber at one end. Into this chamber is inserted a bullet or shotgun shell. The cartridge must be waterproofed which is no easy task. Glue or nail varnish are usually effective, but even so a cartridge will often leak and fail to fire. However, a bangstick rammed against an incoming shark will, if it detonates at the right angle, maim or kill the shark, as the expanding gases rupture the skin and enter the body with great destructive force. Needless to say, the chances of hitting a charging shark in the right place are slim and the bangstick is an unreliable weapon at best. It can even be dangerous, simply because it tends to bolster the confidence of the person carrying it. And it is all too easy to accidentally shoot oneself with it. Given all this, I was not surprised when Tiny handed me a short steel pole to fend off sharks, while he kept the bangstick for himself.

We arrived at the whistle buoy in an unpleasantly choppy sea. As Tiny and I kitted up, the boat lurched back and forth in the swell. I was anxious to get below the surface into the calm depths, but also quite apprehensive about seeing sharks. Tiny jumped in before me and glimpsed a small tiger shark moving off into the distance. By the time I got in it had gone. We descended to the bottom and looked around. It was a flat, featureless terrain of small, broken-up coral formations. There were hardly any fish. The flatness of the terrain and the clarity of the water made me feel exposed and vulnerable. At any moment I expected to see a bulky shadow in the distance. Tiny took his diving knife out of its sheath and started to bang it against his tank in the hope that the sound would attract a shark. The loud clanging noise carried into the gloom. I secretly wished he would stop making so much noise, and I was even beginning to hope that nothing would turn up. Tiny carried on clanging his knife against his tank – a trick that I have since adopted with considerable success. However, on this occasion no shark appeared. A large barracuda, of about 1.5 metres (5 feet) put in an appearance, hovering above us and gazing down with its large, dark eyes. Then it swam off with leisurely grace.

We did not try again. Tiny's boat was heavily booked by regular divers. And anyway, we all knew that to repeat the attempt, based largely on hearsay, was more than likely to be a waste of time. So my interest in sharks was still largely frustrated. I could imagine these powerful animals cruising offshore, occasionally venturing into water a metre (3 feet) or less in depth. But I had not seen them. It was becoming clear to me that sharks are a great deal rarer, and shyer, than most people imagine – something that subsequent experience has confirmed.

Talking to local fishermen tended to be disappointing. They could tell me of the fat tiger sharks they pulled in off deep-water wrecks, or the heavy-headed bull sharks they caught in inshore waters. But I wanted to see the animals in their own realm. The carcasses that the fishermen eagerly displayed I could only view with regret. The sagas of how the shark had been caught, and of the great struggles that had taken place before these animals were gaffed and landed, I listened to with silent indignation.

Though sharks were already a passion, it would be six years before I actually dived with large sharks and managed to photograph them at close range. This fulfilment of my ambitions happened at Long Island in the Bahamas – a story that I will take up in Chapter Three.

At that early stage, even if I had found a shark that was willing to pose, I doubt if I could have obtained any good photographs. I still had a great deal to learn about both scuba diving and photography – and about doing the two things at the same time. The word 'SCUBA' stands for Self-Contained Underwater Breathing Apparatus. The scuba diver is carrying his air supply in the tank, or tanks, on his back. Scuba diving became possible thanks to Jacques Cousteau and Emile Gagnan, who invented the demand valve, or regulator, in 1943. This device automatically provides the diver with air from his compressed air tanks on inhalation (i.e. on demand). This air is provided at the same pressure as the water surrounding the diver, so the greater the depth of the water, the greater the pressure of the air provided by the regulator. If the air was not at the same pressure as his surroundings then he would not be able to breathe: his lungs would collapse under the pressure.

With the invention of scuba diving, the underwater swimmer became comparatively liberated in the water compared with the bottom-trudging hard-hat diver of old, whose air supply was pumped down from the surface. The diving mask restores the scuba diver's vision, and the fins greatly increase swimming ability. (Though he is still slower than virtually everything he encounters that can move at all!) A wet suit provides warmth in all but the coldest waters – where a dry suit is an alternative. The wet suit is a body-hugging garment, usually made out of neoprene rubber, which allows a little water to enter the suit. This water is then trapped between the suit and the skin and warmed by the heat of the body. On the other hand, a dry suit is completely waterproof and the diver wears heavy woollen undergarments to keep him warm. Dry suits are unnecessary, except in very cold water, and most divers use wet suits.

The neoprene material of the wet suit contains millions of tiny gas bubbles and these help to make the diver buoyant. Therefore the diver needs a weight belt, equipped with lead weights, to allow him to descend. Most divers strive to be neutrally buoyant, or a little heavy underwater. The deeper the diver goes, the more compressed the bubbles in his wet suit become, and the heavier, or less buoyant, he is. In the old days, a diver used to have something of a problem. If he was going to make a deep dive, then at his maximum depth he might not need any weights at all, thanks to this compression effect. However, he would need weights to get down there in the first place. Often this would result in a diver being very negatively buoyant at depth. This made swimming difficult and was also somewhat alarming. I well remember, in the early dives, having to haul myself up after a deep dive, using the coral wall as a ladder. Nowadays a simple device has solved this problem. This is called an adjustable buoyancy lifejacket, or ABLJ. Air can be introduced into it via a hose on the regulator, to increase buoyancy, or expelled into the open water at the touch of a button. Now it is easy to be exactly the right weight at any depth. As well as making diving generally far less strenuous, this has been a major improvement for underwater photographers. By giving the diver much greater control over buoyancy, the ABLJ allows the diver to hover in position and concentrate on taking pictures.

Needless to say, scuba diving has its drawbacks. There are two major problems that arise from breathing air under pressure. The first is the problem of decompression sickness (or 'the bends') and the second is nitrogen narcosis, or what Cousteau, with his characteristic turn of phrase, called 'rapture of the depths'. Decompression sickness is caused by the absorption of nitrogen into the body tissues – the greater the depth, the more is absorbed. A diver plans his dive accordingly, knowing how long he can stay at a certain depth without absorbing too much nitrogen. If he stays beyond this limit, then it will be necessary to perform decompression stops before returning to the surface. These stops, at various depths for various times, allow the nitrogen to come out of the body tissues and be expelled from the lungs harmlessly. To ignore the stops is to take a terrible risk, as the nitrogen will form bubbles throughout the body as the diver rises to the surface, and these can cause serious injury or even death. To prevent this, the diver uses an underwater watch to time his dive, and a depth gauge. The deeper the dive, the shorter the time a diver can spend at that depth if he wishes to avoid decompressing. For example, a diver can remain indefinitely in water of less than 9 metres (30 feet) in depth, without having to decompress. If he dives to 20 metres (66 feet), then he will have to begin his return to the surface after forty-five minutes, in order to avoid decompressing. If a diver goes down to 50 metres (165 feet), then he must return after only seven minutes. The various complexities of decompression sickness are not fully understood, and most divers therefore err well on the side of caution, doing decompression stops that are not theoretically necessary.

Nitrogen narcosis is the other major problem that is encountered during deep diving. Nitrogen, breathed under pressure, has a drug-like effect. Different people react differently. One person might be heavily 'narked' at 20 metres (66 feet) while another might not notice any effect until 40 metres (132 feet). Symptoms also vary. One person might feel completely at ease – invincible even – when he should, in fact, be at his most cautious. Another might lose all sense of direction and become helpless. Divers under the influence of narcosis have been known to remove their mouthpiece and offer their air supply to a passing fish. Diving below 50 metres (165 feet) multiplies the problems: placing extra limitations on time due to decompression requirements, and increasing the risk of narcosis. Sports divers are therefore advised not to dive beyond 50 metres. But

Close approaches by sharks on divers can be disconcerting, especially if not seen until the last moment. Here, in the Bahamas, a Caribbean reef shark sneaks up on Jason Burrows from behind.

some of the most exciting spectacles are to be found at these depths. I have done many dives to 50 metres and beyond, and am lucky that my own reactions to narcosis do not put me at any great risk. Whereas most people tend to gain a feeling of immortality I do not. Rather, I become more aware of my surroundings and extra safety-conscious: which is not to say that I am not narked. At 70 metres (230 feet) the narcosis can be quite heavy – I will be checking my depth gauge, watch and air supply every couple of seconds!

Diving to depths beyond 50 metres (165 feet) requires considerable experience and is not something to be undertaken lightly. To dive beyond 70 metres (230 feet) is foolhardy at best. Not only do the problems of narcosis and decompression mount, but oxygen can become spontaneously poisonous at such high pressure. Breathing compressed air at 80 metres (265 feet) allows a very high concentration of oxygen to appear in the blood and brain. At these concentrations oxygen is toxic: the diver convulses and loses consciousness.

The dangers of scuba diving are such that the golden rule of diving is: Never Dive Alone. But for the photograper, this is a difficult rule to follow. The trouble is that the diver is concerned with travelling along underwater and seeing a variety of things. The underwater photographer, however, is concerned with finding something to photograph, and then sticking with that. Thus if a diver is teamed up with a photographer, the result is misery for both: the diver is continually delayed by the photographer and the photographer is rushed by the diver. Certainly the photographer's problem can be solved by teaming up with another photographer, but this rarely works well: they end up fighting each other for the same subject. Thus many serious underwater photographers prefer to dive alone, despite the increased risk.

But there is an advantage in diving alone, because the shyness of the animals is often lessened. This is not only true for such small creatures as reef fish, but also for the larger animals, such as sharks, that one so rarely encounters. If there are two or more divers together, a shark may well keep its distance. However, if you are alone, a shy animal may swim up to you for a quick look.

Given the inherent problems of diving, it is hardly surprising that underwater photography is a frustrating activity. The technical difficulty of getting a sophisticated piece of equipment like a camera to operate underwater is an additional obstacle to be overcome. There are two basic camera systems available. The most popular and easy to operate is an amphibious camera – one that is specifically designed to go underwater. Over the years, Nikon have been marketing a series of such cameras that share the generic name 'Nikonos'. The latest versions rely heavily on electronics, whereas the earlier models were entirely mechanical. Compact and easy to operate, with lenses of the highest optical quality, the various Nikonos systems are the backbone of the underwater photographer's equipment.

The main drawback of the Nikonos system is that the camera is not a reflex camera – you cannot look through a viewfinder and see what the lens 'sees'. The photographer must estimate the distance of the subject from the camera and then set the focus accordingly. This is not too much of a problem when wide-angle lenses are being used, as the great depth of field that such lenses offer make accurate distance-estimation less critical. However, there is a whole range of subjects which the Nikonos system is barely able to manage: namely, free-swimming animals that are not very large (less than a metre – 3 feet – in length) and not very far away (less than about 1.5 metres – 5 feet). While a wide-angle lens will ensure the subject is in focus, it will appear tiny on the film because of the great angle of the lens. A longer lens – one that would allow the subject to take up a greater area of the final picture – has correspondingly less depth of field, and so diminishes the chances of getting the subject in focus, especially if it is moving.

The alternative is to take a land-based single-lens reflex camera and put it into a waterproof housing. This camera will allow you to focus on the subject, and see exactly what is going to be recorded on film. The disadvantages of such systems are cost (for both the camera and the housing), and the fact that they tend to be bulky and awkward to operate underwater. Nevertheless they allow you to concentrate on many subjects that the Nikonos cannot handle very well. Given the advantages and disadvantages of each system, most professionals tend to use both, oscillating between the two as the situation demands.

One of the earliest lessons to be learned in underwater photography is that water absorbs light. At 60 metres (200 feet), in even the clearest water on a sunny day, the seascape is no brighter than twilight on land. At 200 metres (660 feet), it is dark. Not only does water absorb light, but it absorbs some wavelengths more readily than others. The first to go is the red range of the spectrum. A red swimsuit looks dull grey-brown at 5 metres (16 feet), because most of the red wavelengths, that would normally reflect from the fabric, are absent in the light that filters down from above. By 10 metres (33 feet) orange wavelengths in the light have also been absorbed. By 20 metres (66 feet) the yellows have gone. At 25 metres (82 feet) green has been absorbed, leaving only blue and black.

Photographing at depth, using only the available light, produces poor images with very little contrast and muted colours. The solution is to add artificial light to the subject – in other words, use electronic flash (or, as it is often called, a strobe). A strobe will restore the colours of the subject and vastly improve the quality of the image. However, even the largest of strobes are effective only over a short distance underwater, as their light is also absorbed. Beyond 2.5 metres (8 feet), a strobe is all but useless, the ideal distance being little more than a metre (3 feet). Furthermore, strobes are slow to recharge: six or seven seconds is a typical recharge time. If a shark is swimming towards you and you are using a strobe, you will probably only get one shot of it before it swims away: by the time the strobe has recharged, the shark will almost certainly have left. I have often waited to photograph an approaching shark, mentally willing it to come closer before it turns off, but knowing that if I wait too long it will probably turn away before I take the shot. If I do not release the shutter until I see it beginning its turn, then it is too late – the picture will be of a retreating shark. Fairly early on I realized that this was a dilemma that I would have to resolve if I was going to photograph these animals successfully. In the end, I found that there is no golden rule – just hard-won experience and a sense of timing. And the patience to try again when it does not work.

It might be thought that it would be possible to put a telephoto lens onto an underwater camera and photograph sharks from a distance, making them appear closer through sheer lens-power. However, the same problem arises as with the telephoto lenses on land – they cannot be used on hazy or misty days because they 'concentrate' the particles or water droplets in the air. Although they pull the subject closer, the amount of air between the camera and the subject remains the same, so they intensify its effect. Even the clearest seawater is filled with organic material and a subject photographed 6 metres (20 feet) away would be very indistinct and lacking in detail.

Given all these problems, it soon became clear to me that the best distance to photograph a shark is from 1.5 metres (5 feet) away – or less. Here, the strobe can do its work, and the body of water between the subject and the camera is kept to a minimum. The question is: how do you get sharks, which are normally shy, but potentially dangerous, close enough to be photographed?

One of the first obstacles to be overcome is one's own fear. There are dangers, of course, but it is important to get them in proportion, and to understand which circumstances add up to a really hazardous situation. This requires a certain amount of understanding of the creatures concerned: knowing what they eat, how they hunt, and what makes them 'tick', is the key to approaching them in safety.

When I was eleven years old I witnessed a comparatively minor incident that demonstrates this well – and shows the degree of fear that sea creatures can unjustifiably evoke. My family and I were on a beach in a small cove in Bermuda. There were a few coral heads just offshore and about twenty people were in the water, swimming and snorkelling. Then someone spotted a barracuda of about a metre (3 feet) in length hovering just above the sand. Word got around that this vicious animal was lying in wait for a mouthful of tourist and, with that, everyone rushed out of the water. Few ventured back in for the rest of the afternoon. I now know that such a reaction was completely unnecessary. Barracuda look extremely menacing: sleek and powerful with large mouths and prominent teeth. However they do not pose a threat in clear water because they feed on fish smaller than themselves. In murky water the situation is different. A piece of jewellery or a ring can flash like the side of a fish. Then a barracuda can attack because of mistaken identity.

The fear that people have for barracuda is interesting because it has some features in common with their fear of sharks. Fishermen will tell you that creatures such as barracuda and moray eels are extremely dangerous. Both have razor-sharp teeth that can inflict serious injury. However, a fisherman's experience is of these animals as they fight for their lives, biting and writhing on the end of the line. Not surprisingly, when they are brought up onto the boat, they continue to struggle and will bite anything in range. This tells you nothing about how an unmolested barracuda or moray eel will behave in its natural environment. Similarly, spear-fishermen frequently warn of the dangerousness of these animals, and tell you how often they try to bite. Invariably, it turns out that the animal did indeed try to bite the spear-fishermen – after he had jabbed a spear into it. An understandable reaction.

The same is often true of sharks. A fisherman's encounters with these animals are generally confined to their death struggles on the end of the line, or their snapping and twisting when he stabs them with a gaff. Thus the myth of the shark's viciousness is perpetuated. Indeed, fishermen are often astounded at divers who happily dive in 'shark-infested' waters.

If nothing else, I hope that the story of my own encounters with sharks will help to improve their badly tarnished public image – for sharks are desperately in need of our respect, and our protection. Many are the victims of disgraceful, unregulated fishing methods. One appalling incident occurred quite recently, off the coast of California. A species of thresher shark, the 'common thresher' *Alopias vulpinus*, was, until November 1986, as common as its name suggests, in the offshore waters around Los Angeles. During the spring and summer, these threshers are thought to migrate northwards in considerable numbers along the western coast of the United States, while in the autumn they return to southern waters. That November, gill-net fishermen, using a spotter plane, saw an enormous school of thresher sharks moving southwards down the Californian coast. Threshers are unfortunate enough to be considered edible, and on spotting the school of migrating threshers, a dozen gill-net boats converged and spent two weeks catching the threshers by the ton. It remains to be seen whether this decimated school was the backbone of the population, and whether that population will ever recover. It would be a tragedy if these threshers have been exterminated, for they are remarkable, if little-studied sharks. They use their extraordinarily elongated tails as weapons, swimming through a shoal of fish and lashing their tails back and forth to stun their victims.

The way in which thresher sharks catch their prey is intriguing, and a striking example of how these superb predators have become adapted for their particular way of life. But threshers are just one group among the 350 or so species of sharks alive today. Each species is a fascinating story in its own right, as are the sharks' closest relatives – the skates, rays and chimaeras. Before describing my own travels in search of sharks, it may be worthwhile to look more closely at the group as a whole, and at their relatives, in order to appreciate the way of life and complex adaptations of these magnificent creatures.

CHAPTER TWO

—THE—
SHARK FILE

Most people have a good idea of what a shark looks like — more or less like a fish, but then again, not *quite* like a fish. At least, not like a typical fish. We can recognize some deep-rooted essence that links a salmon to a stickleback, a mackerel to a perch — but sharks are somehow different. When we think of a salmon or a mackerel we think of it in terms of its shape and colour. But when we think of a shark we tend to think in other terms — terms that relate, not so much to the details of its appearance as to our own deep-rooted reactions to it. It is sinister, menacing, dangerous. However unjustified such descriptions may be, they illustrate an almost instinctive thought that we have about sharks. They are not the same as other fish, and it is not a difference of degree, but of kind.

Sharks seem to us unknowable, mysterious. There can be nothing mysterious about a salmon or a perch because we do not ask strange questions about them — they are just fish. Somehow we tend to think that there is a deeper level at which sharks are to be understood, that there is more going on. This, perhaps, is why some people become obsessed with sharks — obsessed with studying them, catching them, killing them — even photographing them.

However confused our thinking is about sharks, the instinctive level at which we separate them from other fish is, basically, correct. Sharks, unlike most fish, do not possess a bony skeleton. Instead, the skeleton of sharks is made out of cartilage, a tough rubbery semi-rigid material which contains a special protein, collagen. We have areas of cartilage in our own skeleton — at the tip of the nose, in the external ear flaps, and at the end of each bone, helping the joints to work smoothly. As embryos, we have even more cartilage — every bone in the body is made of it. But as we grow, the cartilage is gradually 'ossified', or turned into bone, by the formation within it of hard mineral deposits (calcium phosphate). The same is true of all vertebrates (mammals, birds, reptiles, amphibians and fish) with the sole exception of the sharks and their allies, where the cartilage stays unchanged. Though the cartilage of a shark's body is strengthened in some parts by calcium deposits, for example in the vertebral column, and though this parallels bone in terms of functional strengthening, it is not true bone.

The possession of a cartilaginous skeleton, rather than one made out of bone, is a basic feature, not only of sharks, but also of skates, rays and an odd group of deep-water fish called rat-fish or chimaeras. Because of this unique feature, they are classed together in Class

Chondrichthyes, better known as the cartilaginous fish.

The rest of the world's fish fall into three major groups: the jawless fish, the ray-finned fish and the lobe-finned fish. Of these the most abundant by far are the ray-finned fish, especially the group of ray-fins known as teleosts, which account for 20,750 species – over 96% of the total of all fish – and include virtually all the fish with which we are familiar.

The ray-finned fish and lobe-finned fish are sometimes referred to collectively as the 'bony fish' but this name is now going out of use, because it is considered misleading: jawless fish (such as the lampreys) also have bone. The sharks, rays and chimaeras are alone in their preference for cartilage.

Because cartilage precedes bone in most vertebrates, it used to be assumed that fish with cartilaginous skeletons were ancestral to fish with bony skeletons – making sharks and their allies more 'primitive' than the other groups of fish. However, the very first fish appeared 150 million years *before* the first sharks – and these first fish had bone. So it is more likely that cartilaginous fish evolved from fish with bones, and for some reason abandoned the ossification process.

There is no denying the great antiquity of sharks and other cartilaginous fish – the first sharks are recorded from the Devonian period, 350 million years ago, and, superficially at least, they have changed very little since then. But this does not mean that the present-day species are archaic, unsophisticated survivors of an earlier era. The cartilaginous fish that we see today have been around for hundreds of millions of years, competing with, and feeding on, a

The Cartilaginous Fish

The three groups of cartilaginous fish are the chimaeras, the skates and rays and the sharks, classed together in the Class Chondrichthyes. All possess a cartilaginous skeleton and the males have claspers. There are some differences between them, however. Chimaeras, like the teleosts, have a gill cover which means that only one gill opening is visible externally. In the sharks, skates and rays, the gill openings (usually five) are all visible on the outside of the body.

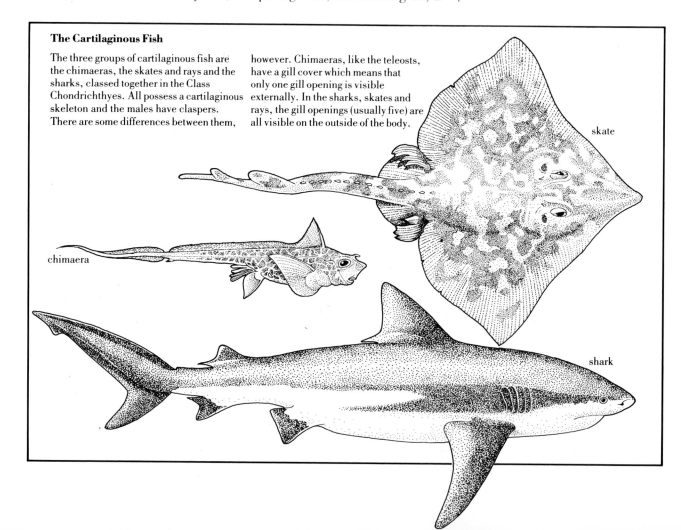

skate

chimaera

shark

The spotted eagle ray *Aetobatus narinari* is one of the more spectacular members of the ray family. This individual, photographed in the Coral Sea beyond the Great Barrier Reef, had a wingspan of 2 metres (6 feet 6 inches) and was swimming in large circles in the sandy area inside a reef. I stalked it for many minutes and then hid behind the coral head in the foreground when I saw the ray swimming towards me. By good luck it did not see me and I got one shot of it before it sped off.

wide range of ever-evolving animals. They must have got something right. The secrets of their success will emerge as we look in detail at the three groups of cartilaginous fish.

Of all the cartilaginous fish, the most curious by far are the rat-fish or chimaeras. They have evolved many features that separate them from the sharks, skates and rays, and have a peculiar, science-fiction look about them, with bulging iridescent eyes, a pointed snout, large wing-like fins and a long tapering whip-lash of a tail. It is the tail that earned them the unendearing name of 'rat-fish'. Known scientifically as the Holocephalans, they first appeared some 150 million years ago, in the Jurassic era.

Unlike other cartilaginous fish, chimaeras have small mouths that possess lips, and their teeth are fused to form a hard 'beak', which enables them to crack open shellfish and other food items. It was probably the combination of a bird-like beak with a fish's body and a rat's tail that first invited comparison with the *chimaera* of Greek legend – an incongruous monster with the body of a goat, the head of a roaring lion and the tail of a serpent.

For all their oddities, chimaeras have one feature in common with most other fish – a thick flap of toughened skin that covers the gills, known as an operculum. This is lacking in other cartilaginous fish, so a row of parallel gill slits can be seen along the side of the body in sharks, or underneath the body in the case of the skates and rays. As this shared feature indicates, the sharks, rays and skates are much more closely related to each other than they are to the chimaeras, and they are sometimes referred to collectively as the Elasmobranchs.

Yet despite their affinities with the sharks, the rays and skates form a distinctive subgroup of their own, the Order Rajiformes. The majority are found in the shallow waters of temperate and tropical seas, and they have a worldwide distribution. As their flattened bodies indicate, they were originally adapted to life on the seabed – a parallel development to that in the teleost fish which produced the plaice, sole and flounder. Most rays and skates still feed on small invertebrates, such as crabs, molluscs and worms, that they dig up out of the mud or sand of the seafloor. But some have abandoned this way of life for a more active, roving existence, and a few, such as the sawfish, have reverted to an almost shark-like body shape.

The most spectacular member of the Rajiformes is the gigantic manta ray *Manta birostris* of tropical seas: the largest recorded manta, caught in the Bahamas, had a wingspan of 6.7 metres (22 feet) and weighed 1360 kg (3000 lb). Despite their great size, manta rays are entirely harmless, for they are filter feeders, sustained by tiny organisms that they sift from the water as they flap slowly along. In the sea, great size is often linked with a diet made up of the smallest ocean creatures, floating inhabitants of the surface waters known as 'plankton'. The explanation for this paradox is the superabundance of the plankton, and the ease of collecting it if some sort of sieving arrangement can be achieved. All ocean creatures ultimately depend on the plankton for food, but most are part of a long 'food chain', in which they prey on smaller species, and are eaten, in turn, by larger predators. Giant filter feeders, such as the blue whale, the whale shark and the manta ray, have simply cut out the ocean's 'middle-men', and are exploiting the plankton directly. The manta ray filters out the plankton with its gills, although it also has a pair of fleshy paddle-like appendages on either side of the mouth that can scoop up passing fish to supplement its diet.

Photographing manta rays underwater is said to be one of the great thrills for an underwater photographer – I have yet to succeed. Although I have seen mantas occasionally, they have almost always been far off, moving gracefully but purposefully away. Except once – and this was by far the most exasperating episode I have ever had with a manta. It was in the Red Sea on the Sanganeb reef. I had just finished a deep dive, and was snorkelling along the coral wall, where the water plunges vertically to great depth. Looking straight down from above the water below is black in colour, but in it I noticed some curious white shapes far away, at a depth of 25 metres (80 feet) or more. I could not make them out at first. There were two pale triangular shapes that pointed away from each other about 5 metres (16 feet) apart and between them, but slightly ahead, two pale bars, shaped like rods parallel to each other. For several seconds I wondered what on earth I was looking at, presuming it to be a group of animals moving slowly along the reef face. Then, with a start, I realized that I was not looking at several animals, but at one enormous manta. The upper surface of the body of mantas is dark in colour, while the 'wingtips' and the fleshy mouth-parts (which were sticking out, in front of the head) are pale. Thus most of the body, apart from the pale areas, was invisible. The manta was too deep for me to snorkel down to, let alone get a picture of. All I could do was gaze down on it, from above, as it glided, tantalizingly slowly, along the reef wall.

Rays that live on the seabed have developed a variety of defensive measures to protect themselves from predators. Passive measures include a camouflaged colouration, and burying into the sand or mud of the seafloor. More active measures include, among the 'stingrays', a collection of barbed, venomous spines in the tail. People who wade in shallow waters in the tropics run the risk of being severely injured by a stingray, should they tread on one. Yet these spines are treated with contempt by several species of shark that feed on them, including the great hammerhead *Sphyrna mokarran* which has a particular fondness for stingrays. Indeed, the barbs of their victims are often found embedded in the jaws of hammerheads, and one was reported to have had no less than ninety-six barbs stuck in its jaw, mouth and head!

George Williams, a professional fisherman from Key Largo in the Florida Keys, once told me an intriguing tale about hammerheads and rays. While fishing the local inshore waters, he noticed several large splashes in the distance, and headed his boat towards the commotion. Arriving at the scene he came across a large hammerhead that appeared to be hunting a good-sized ray. He soon realized however, that the ray was dead and that the shark was not hunting it after all, but playing with it, in much the same way that a cat plays with a dead mouse.

Rays and their allies are generally assumed to have evolved from the same ancestral stock as the sharks, but their fossil record is sparse, since cartilage is very rarely fossilized, and no firm conclusions can be drawn. Only those few features of the body that are mineralized tend to be preserved – the teeth, principally, and the fin spines. Fossil teeth alone are not enough to show how and when the sharks and rays diverged. Fortunately, the anatomy of the living sharks can offer some clues.

Like rays, sharks are thought to have gone through a bottom-dwelling phase in their evolution, although they did not resort to the extreme flattening of the body seen in the rays. During the Permian and Triassic eras (from about 270 to 180 million years ago) it is thought that there were not many free-swimming smaller fish in the seas for sharks to hunt. Thus sharks adapted to feeding on invertebrates – molluscs, crustaceans and worms – that are found on the seafloor. The most striking change which this induced in the early sharks was that the mouth became located on the underside of the head. When the supply of free-swimming bony fish increased, sharks returned to hunting them, but for some reason the mouth remained on the underside of the head. In an active predator like a modern-day shark the obvious place to have the mouth would be at the end of the head, where it is nearest to the prey. Certainly, with the mouth located underneath the head, a shark cannot see what it is biting. But on deeper analysis it seems that this is not such a bad place for the mouth to be after all. Greater streamlining of the front of a shark is possible with the mouth out of the way. But more than that, it is directly behind the nostrils: so the shark can smell what it is about to bite, even if it cannot see it. In the sea, especially in murky water, smell is a much more potent source of information than sight. And again, there are organs on the head of the shark called the ampullae of Lorenzini, that act as electroreceptors. They provide the shark with further sensory information and are found in considerable numbers in front of the mouth.

A classification of modern sharks

This is an abbreviated version of Compagno's classification of modern sharks as it appears in the FAO species catalogue, Vol.4, Part 1 *Sharks of the World* published in 1984.

The symbol * indicates that photographs of representative species are included in this book.

Dogfish sharks (Order Squaliformes) Comprises three families: the BRAMBLE SHARKS (Echinorhinidae); the SPINY DOGFISH (Squalidae) and the ROUGH SHARKS (Oxynotidae). This is a fascinating and divergent group of sharks. Many are deepwater forms known only from occasional specimens caught in deepwater nets.

Frilled and cow sharks (Order Hexanchiformes) There are two families: the single, primitive FRILLED SHARK (Chlamydoselachidae) and the COW SHARKS (Hexanchidae). Most cow sharks favour deep water.

Horn or bullhead sharks (Order Heterodontiformes) During the day they hide under kelp or in rock gullies, becoming active at night. Found in Pacific and Indian Oceans from surface shallows down to a few hundred metres. Feed on sea urchins, gastropods, crustaceans, polychaetes, abalone and occasional bony fish.

Ground sharks (Order Carcharhiniformes) There are eight families: the CATSHARKS (Scyliorhinidae) with fifteen genera, many of which are deepwater forms; the FINBACK CATSHARKS (Proscyllidae), with four poorly known genera with small individuals inhabiting deep water; the single FALSE CATSHARK (Pseudotriatidae); the single BARBELED HOUNDSHARK (Leptochariidae); the SMOOTH-HOUNDS (Triakidae); with nine genera; the WEASEL SHARKS (Hemigaleidae), with about seven recognized species; the GREY or REQUIEM SHARKS (Carcharhinidae), with genera abundant in tropical and temperate seas; and the HAMMERHEAD SHARKS (Sphyrnidae), with two genera instantly recognized by the lateral expansions of the head.

Saw sharks (Order Pristiophoriformes) Small, rarely over 1 metre (3 feet), and widely distributed. Range from shallow to deep water (2,900 feet/915 metres) and occasionally form groups to feed. Five species.

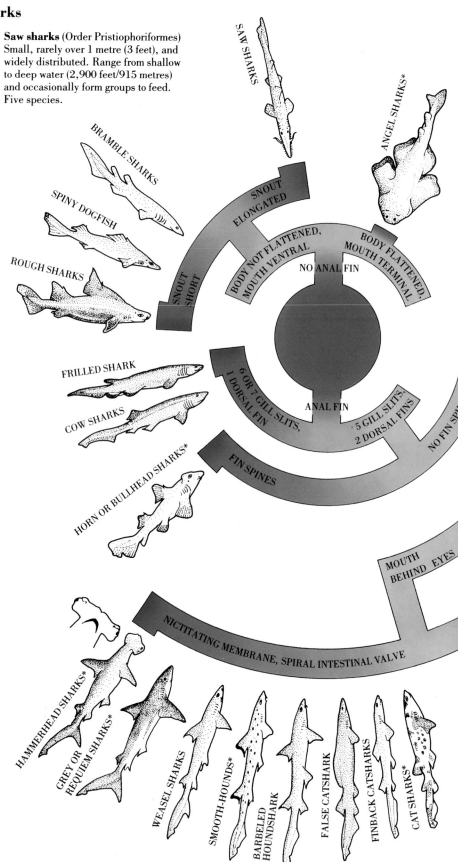

Angel sharks (Order Squatiniformes) Unusual-looking sharks with flattened body often mistaken for rays. Lie on sandy or muddy bottoms, sometimes partly bury themselves in substrate. Twelve known species ranging from cool temperate to tropical waters.

Carpet sharks (Order Orectolobiformes) There are seven families: the COLLARED CARPET SHARKS (Parascyllidae), little known bottom dwellers less than 1 metre (3 feet) confined to deep water; BLIND SHARKS (Brachaeluridae), small

and harmless bottom dwellers from Australia; the WOBBEGONGS (Orectolobidae), found in great numbers off Australia and New Guinea; the BAMBOO SHARKS (Hemiscyllidae), with two genera; the single ZEBRA SHARK (Stegostomidae); the NURSE SHARKS (Ginglymostomatidae), which are large, sluggish bottom dwellers of the Atlantic, Indian and Pacific Oceans with distinct barbels on the snout and powerful jaws; and the single WHALE SHARK (Rhincodontidae), the largest fish in the sea.

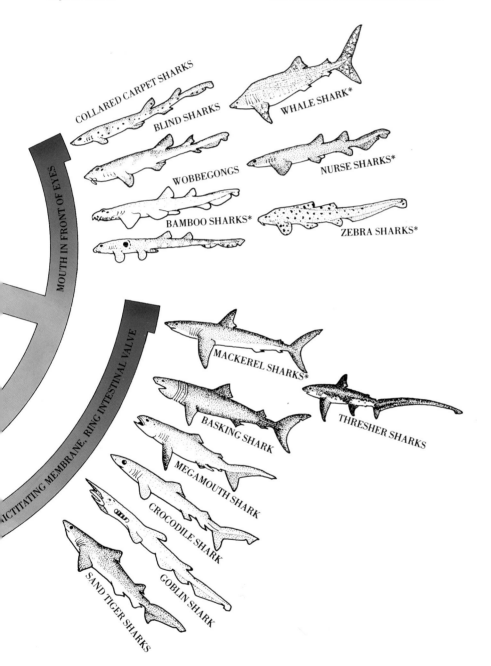

Mackerel sharks (Order Lamniformes) There are seven families: SAND TIGER SHARKS (Odontaspidae), with five species all of which are large piscivorous sharks preferring cool waters; the single, extraordinary GOBLIN SHARK (Mitsukurinidae) about which little is known; the single CROCODILE SHARK (Pseudocarchariidae), a small oceanic shark with enormous eyes and large, thin teeth; the extremely rare MEGAMOUTH SHARK (Megachasmidae), a filter-feeding shark first discovered in 1976; the THRESHER SHARKS (Alopiidae), with three species in which the upper lobe of the tail has become lengthened into a weapon for striking fish; the single BASKING SHARK (Cetorhinidae), a filter feeder growing to perhaps 12 metres (40 feet); and the MACKEREL SHARKS (Lamnidae), which include the infamous great white, two species of porbeagle and two species of mako shark.

The unusual location of the mouth in sharks once led to the belief that a shark could not actually bite something directly in front of it. Indeed, one myth was that a shark has to roll onto its back in order to bite at all. This idea harks back to the notion of a shark being 'primitive': imagine an animal so poorly designed that it has to turn upside-down in order to feed! Observation and filming of feeding sharks has long since disproved this. The upper jaw of a shark is not actually fused to the braincase. A shark is perfectly capable of biting something directly in front of it: the jaws can be thrust forward into an almost terminal position, while the snout is elevated out of the way.

The deadly effectiveness of a shark's bite depends not just on its jaw-action but also on the structure of its teeth. Sharks have evolved a wide variety of tooth designs, and it is often possible to identify the species of a shark from one tooth, or even the fragment of a tooth, so characteristic are certain types. The shape is appropriate for the prey on which the shark usually feeds. For example, a shark that feeds on molluscs needs teeth that are capable of crushing the hard, chalky shells of these animals. The teeth of the nurse shark *Ginglymostoma cirratum* are so adapted. Sharks such as the shortfin mako *Isurus oxyrinchus*, that feed on small, free-swimming fish which they swallow whole, often have long, thin teeth with which to impale their prey. By contrast, those sharks that tend to bite chunks out of prey, rather than swallow the prey intact, usually have broad, serrated teeth. They include the most dangerous of sharks – the great white shark *Carcharodon carcharias*, the tiger shark *Galeocerdo cuvieri*, the great hammerhead *Sphyrna mokarran*, and the larger members of the requiem shark group, such as the bull shark *Carcharhinus leucas* and the dusky shark *C. obscurus*. All these are large and aggressive hunters that feed on other large animals, and to whom a human being is a potential meal.

A shark's teeth are not permanent, as ours are, but are continually being replaced by new teeth that develop below them in the jaw (see page 30). This means that a shark's tooth shape can change as it grows older. Mako sharks, when they get very large, lose the slender teeth of their youth and gain much broader, though unserrated teeth. They are presumably no longer feeding on small fish, but hunting larger prey. Similarly, juvenile great white sharks have long, slender teeth that are like those of makos, except for the serrations. At this stage of its life, the great white shark is too small to feed by taking great chunks out of large animals, and is subsisting on smaller fish.

Surprising as it may seem, the skin of a shark is closely related to its teeth. If you run your hand along the side of a dead shark from head to tail, the skin feels quite smooth. Indeed, one species, the silky shark *Carcharhinus falciformis* has derived its common name from the delicate texture of its skin. But rub your hand forward towards the head, and the skin feels rough, like sandpaper. This roughness is due to backward-pointing 'dermal denticles' within the skin. They are formed in the same way as the teeth in the shark's jaw, and made out of the same materials (see page 30). There are various suggestions as to the purpose of these denticles. In those species where they are large and sharp, they presumably serve to protect the shark from predators. The largest denticles are found in the bramble shark, *Echinorhinus brucus*, which, to all intents and purposes, is covered in a toothy coat. In other species, the dermal denticles may serve to trap a layer of water and so reduce friction between the shark's skin and the water around it, making movement through the water less strenuous.

Efficient locomotion is something that sharks are supremely good at, and they have different modes of swimming, suited to the needs of the moment. Often when looking from above at a shark swimming, a snake-like body motion is noticeable: a wave passes down the length of the shark and culminates in a sideways beat of the tail. The whole body is involved in a steady, sinuous swimming movement. When cruising along, this wavy body motion serves them well, but for rapid swimming a different approach is needed. If they become excited, certain species can stiffen the body so that the tail beats more independently of it, and then they can dash with incredible speed. This is possible because the skin of sharks is elastic in nature and muscles within the body are actually attached directly to it, rather than to the skeleton. When those on one side contract, those on the other side of the body stretch. Relaxation of the contracted muscles allows the stretched skin on the opposite side to pull the body back from its bent position. When a shark is swimming slowly, the skin is supple and bends with the waves that pass down towards the tail. However, when it accelerates, and those muscular waves become faster, the internal pressure of the body fluids increases as they are pushed against each side of the skin. This actually causes the skin to become stiffer. The result is that the body bends back and forth less, with a greater percentage of the total wave being focused in the tail. The 'stiffened dash' that this produces is particularly noticeable in the requiem sharks.

The fastest sharks of all are members of the mackerel shark family (Lamnidae), which have many features designed for unbridled speed. The shortfin mako *Isurus oxyrinchus* is the culmination of such features: the snout is pointed and the body heavy-set – packed with muscle. Just before the tail is a feature called the keel (see page 34). This acts to separate the body from the tail, and prevents a wavy swimming motion. Rather, the tail beats independently of the body and gives a mackerel shark a very different swimming motion to other sharks.

Regardless of the details of swimming style, all movement depends ultimately on muscle contractions, and any shark's locomotion is only as efficient as the muscles that produce it. Muscle performance is closely related to body temperature: a cold muscle performs badly compared with a warm one. This creates a difficulty, because all sharks are poikilothermic, or 'cold-blooded': in other words, the temperature of the body is basically the same as the external environment. They cannot generate heat metabolically by 'burning off' fat stores, as mammals such as whales and dolphins can. Furthermore, the little heat generated by muscular movement tends to be lost through the gills: this is an area where many small blood vessels come in contact with seawater, and a great deal of heat escapes from them. However, some sharks, notably the mackerel sharks, have a limited ability to raise their body temperature above that of the surroundings. They have modified the system in which blood is supplied to the gills so as to reduce heat loss, and can therefore conserve the heat produced by muscle action. These measures are sufficient to maintain a body temperature of up to 10°C

The skin and teeth of sharks

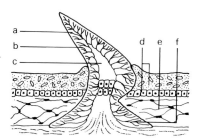

◀▼The skin of sharks is immensely tough and covered in dermal denticles or placoid scales. The cross-section, *left*, shows the typical structure where **a** = enamel-like outer surface, **b** = dentine, **c** = pulp cavity, **d** = epidermis, **e** = dermis and **f** = basal plate (after Steel).

The denticles can serve to trap a layer of water around the body of the shark, *below*. This 'envelope' reduces resistance with seawater.

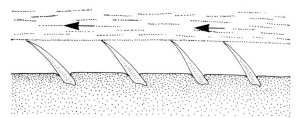

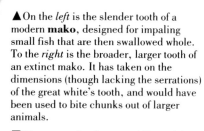

▶This jaw, approximately two-thirds life size, is from a **shortfin mako**. Long, slender teeth are found in the middle of both the upper and lower jaws. They impale the small fish on which the mako feeds. Towards the sides of the jaws the teeth are somewhat more squat, though no less sharp. They serve to cut up pieces of food.

▲On the *left* is the slender tooth of a modern **mako**, designed for impaling small fish that are then swallowed whole. To the *right* is the broader, larger tooth of an extinct mako. It has taken on the dimensions (though lacking the serrations) of the great white's tooth, and would have been used to bite chunks out of larger animals.

▼The **nurse shark** can rapidly suck in water and take bony fish into its mouth, a trick that makes slender grasping teeth unnecessary. Its teeth are flattened into a cobbled pavement-like structure. This design enables the nurse shark to feed on animals such as snails, lobsters, crabs and sea urchins. The teeth crush through the tough defences of its victims.

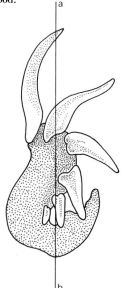

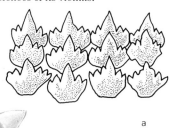

▲This cross-section through the mako jaw shows the formation of new teeth. These develop inside the jaw and then move up to the apex before eventually being lost. The rate of tooth replacement varies with different species. The system is highly efficient since lost and broken teeth constitute no problem to sharks. This method also allows the tooth design of sharks to be modified to suit changes in their diets as they increase in size.

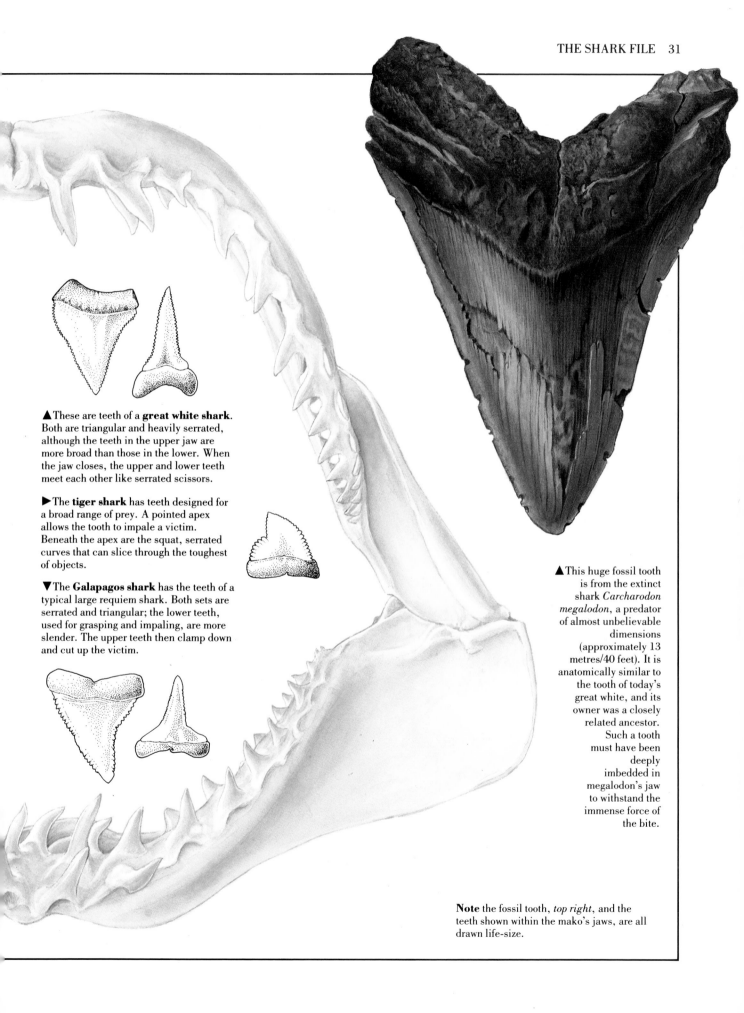

▲These are teeth of a **great white shark**. Both are triangular and heavily serrated, although the teeth in the upper jaw are more broad than those in the lower. When the jaw closes, the upper and lower teeth meet each other like serrated scissors.

▶The **tiger shark** has teeth designed for a broad range of prey. A pointed apex allows the tooth to impale a victim. Beneath the apex are the squat, serrated curves that can slice through the toughest of objects.

▼The **Galapagos shark** has the teeth of a typical large requiem shark. Both sets are serrated and triangular; the lower teeth, used for grasping and impaling, are more slender. The upper teeth then clamp down and cut up the victim.

▲This huge fossil tooth is from the extinct shark *Carcharodon megalodon*, a predator of almost unbelievable dimensions (approximately 13 metres/40 feet). It is anatomically similar to the tooth of today's great white, and its owner was a closely related ancestor. Such a tooth must have been deeply imbedded in megalodon's jaw to withstand the immense force of the bite.

Note the fossil tooth, *top right*, and the teeth shown within the mako's jaws, are all drawn life-size.

higher than that of the surrounding ocean. Such an ability gives mackerel sharks a tremendous advantage over other sharks in colder waters, and members of this family are the apex predators in very cold seas. In the North Pacific, the great white shark *Carcharodon carcharias* penetrates to the southern edge of Alaska, while the salmon shark *Lamna ditropis* is found even further north – up to the Sea of Okhotsk and the Bering Sea. In the North Atlantic, the porbeagle *Lamna nasus* is found far north of Iceland, and in the western parts of the Barents Sea.

Any fast-moving predatory animal needs acute senses and quick reactions. In this, sharks are no exception, but their sensory abilities, particularly their visual powers, have long been a matter of controversy. Scientists first studied the structure of a shark's eyes in the middle of the nineteenth century, but until quite recently most of the work had been done on the eyes of the dogfish, *Squalus acanthias*, a small shark found in great abundance in European waters. This early work suggested that dogfish in particular, and perhaps sharks in general, have extremely poor eyesight. The actual structure of the retina of the dogfish eye was shown to be rather crude in comparison with the eyes of higher vertebrates, such as ourselves. The vision of higher vertebrates depends on two types of light-sensitive cells within the retina: the rods and the cones. Rod cells are highly sensitive to light and can operate in low light levels, whereas cone cells cannot. Rods also have poor resolving power, however – in other words, they are supremely sensitive to variations in light, but cannot record the more subtle details in an object. On the other hand, cone cells, though much less sensitive to light, have tremendous resolving power or 'visual acuity'. They can record an object in great detail. Work on the eye of the dogfish showed that they lack cone cells and hence must have poor resolving power.

More recent work has challenged the view that sharks in general have poor eyesight. Certain advanced specializations are known in the shark's eye that seem inappropriate if the vision is in fact so poor. One is the 'tapetum lucidum', a layer of reflective material beneath the retina. A tapetum is seen also in many land animals, including dogs and cats, where it produces a greenish reflection if the animal stares at a light source at night. The tapetum serves the same purpose in sharks as in nocturnal animals such as the cat – improving vision under low-light conditions. Because the tapetum reflects the incoming rays back through the retina, it amplifies the available light. The shark's tapetum is, in a way, more sophisticated than that of land animals, because it can be closed off in certain circumstances – when swimming in shallow, sunlit water, for example.

There is now more direct evidence that many sharks have good vision. Samuel (Sonny) Gruber – who wrote the foreword to this book – has conducted many experiments on the visual systems of the lemon shark *Negaprion brevirostris*. This is an altogether more advanced and impressive animal than the dogfish that earlier scientists examined. Gruber found the lemon shark's retina does indeed contain cone cells as well as rods. Since then he and his colleagues have found cone cells in the eyes of many cartilaginous fish, and further experiments with lemon sharks have shown that they have relatively good visual acuity as well as tremendous light sensitivity.

Looking at the eyes of different sharks, one cannot help but be impressed by the variety. Some, such as the oceanic whitetip *Carcharhinus longimanus*, have eyes which are very small in relation to the total length of the body. Others, such as the sharpnose seven-gill shark *Heptranchias perlo* have enormous eyes. In some species the eyes are round, in others they are elongated. Often, the pupil is visible as a black slit, but in some sharks, the entire eye is black, with the pupil obscured. One of the most remarkable eyes is seen in a species of thresher, the bigeye *Alopias superciliosus*, which is often found in deep water – 500 metres (1,650 feet) or more. Its enormous eyes are mounted in channels in the head that allow it to gaze upwards from a horizontal position. Perhaps it swims along in the depths, locating its prey as a silhouette against the lighter surface.

Although the vision of sharks is better than we first supposed, it is only one feature of a shark's sensory apparatus. After all, some sharks hunt and thrive in murky waters where even the best vision is useless. To guide them in these conditions, sharks have a very acute sense of smell – that is, they can detect water-borne chemicals, in the same way that we pick up chemicals ('scents') in the air. And yet the chemicals they respond to are dissolved in water – so this sense is, in some ways, more akin to our sense of taste.

The sense organs concerned are found in cavities on the head which take in seawater via the nostrils, visible on the underside of the snout. The brain centres that deal with smell (the olfactory centres) are very large and well developed. Indeed, sharks have often been described as 'swimming noses'. Experiments have shown that smell alone is enough for a shark to locate prey – blindfolded sharks have been able to home in on a fish that is giving off no other information. When I am taking down dead fish to feed reef sharks, it never ceases to amaze me how quickly they can smell the bait. A shark that swims by up-current will show little interest in me, in marked contrast to one that passes by down-current, where the smell of the fish has been carried – such a shark will instantly react and come rushing towards me.

The ears of sharks are located on either side of the brain case, though the only sign of them is a small pore for an opening. They are considerably simpler than those of land animals, because hearing in water is an easier business: water conducts sound extremely well, and almost five times faster than air. Fish generally lack the subtleties of terrestrial ears – such as an eardrum – because the underwater world is, in effect, quite loud enough already. In the case of sharks, the most searching auditory experiments have been conducted by Donald Nelson of California State University. Transmitting irregular, low-frequency bursts of sound through an underwater speaker, he has succeeded in attracting reef sharks in considerable numbers on various Pacific reefs. It is probable that the sharks mistake the low frequency pulses as the sound of a struggling, injured fish.

However, the ears of sharks are not the only organs associated with hearing – if, by 'hearing', one means the detection of any water-borne vibration or change in pressure. There are other complex systems whose functions are not fully understood but which undoubtedly sense the pulsations of the seawater all around the shark's body.

The anatomy of sharks

These drawings show both the main external features of sharks and also some of the more remarkable variations on the basic theme. The main figures show a generalized shark.

▶EYES

The **requiem sharks** and **hammerheads** have a third eyelid or nictitating membrane. This is a tough layer of skin that slides across the eye and so protects it when the shark is biting prey.

▶FINS

The propulsive force for swimming is provided by the tail or caudal fin. The tail shown here is heterocercal, the upper lobe being longer than the lower. The pectoral fins counterbalance the slightly downward push of the asymmetrical tail, as well as acting as stabilizers. The dorsal, anal and pelvic fins prevent the body from rolling in response to the beating caudal fin. Many species have stout and often toxic dorsal fin spines for protection against predators. The male intromittant organs or claspers are located between the pelvic fins and are outgrowths from them.

▼HEADS

Sharks display an amazing variety of head shapes. The **saw sharks** have flattened, elongated snouts armed with sharp denticles. The long sensory barbels locate prey and the saw is used to injure the victim. The **shortfin mako** has a pointed snout to maximize speed. The **goblin shark** is a little known deepwater shark. The paddle-like projection above the mouth may serve as a sensory tool for locating prey. The **winged hammerhead's** lateral lobes can be half the total length of the animal.

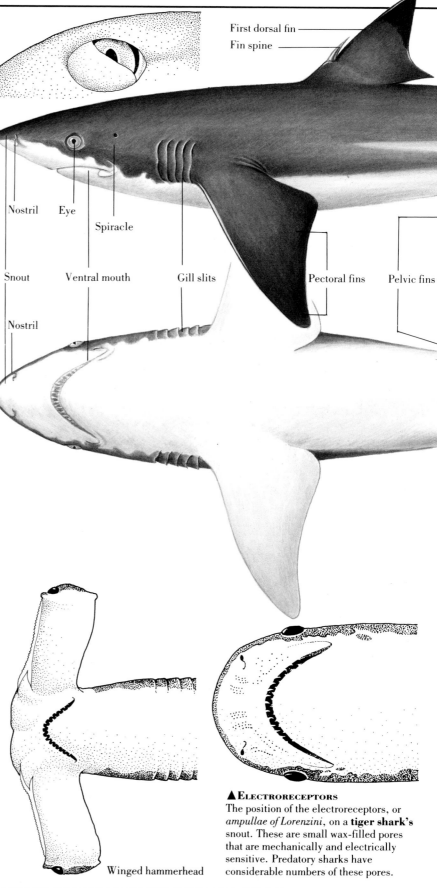

First dorsal fin

Fin spine

Nostril   Eye

Spiracle

Snout   Ventral mouth   Gill slits   Pectoral fins   Pelvic fins

Nostril

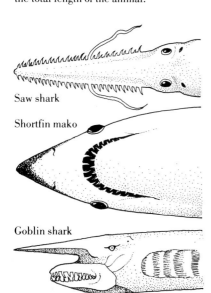

Saw shark

Shortfin mako

Goblin shark

Winged hammerhead

▲ELECTRORECEPTORS

The position of the electroreceptors, or *ampullae of Lorenzini*, on a **tiger shark's** snout. These are small wax-filled pores that are mechanically and electrically sensitive. Predatory sharks have considerable numbers of these pores.

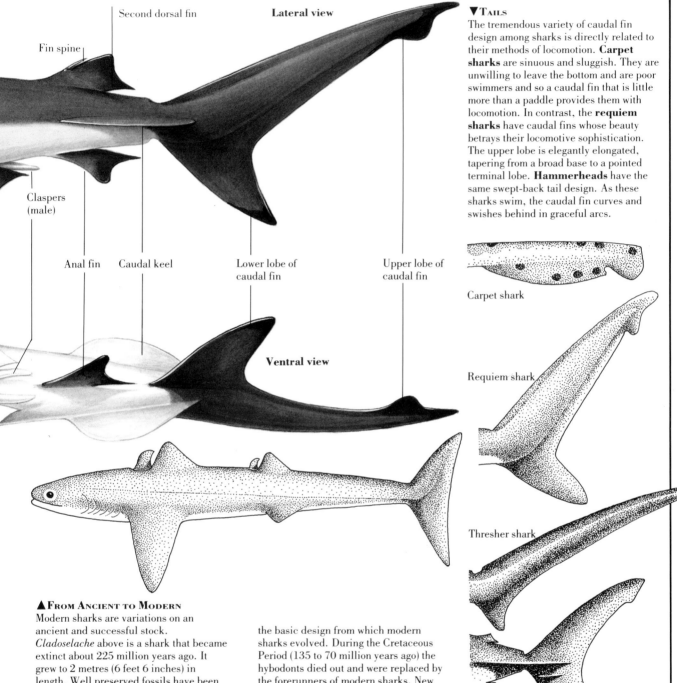

Second dorsal fin

Lateral view

Fin spine

Claspers
(male)

Anal fin   Caudal keel   Lower lobe of   Upper lobe of
                            caudal fin   caudal fin

Ventral view

▼TAILS
The tremendous variety of caudal fin
design among sharks is directly related to
their methods of locomotion. **Carpet
sharks** are sinuous and sluggish. They are
unwilling to leave the bottom and are poor
swimmers and so a caudal fin that is little
more than a paddle provides them with
locomotion. In contrast, the **requiem
sharks** have caudal fins whose beauty
betrays their locomotive sophistication.
The upper lobe is elegantly elongated,
tapering from a broad base to a pointed
terminal lobe. **Hammerheads** have the
same swept-back tail design. As these
sharks swim, the caudal fin curves and
swishes behind in graceful arcs.

Carpet shark

Requiem shark

Thresher shark

Mackerel shark

▲ FROM ANCIENT TO MODERN
Modern sharks are variations on an
ancient and successful stock.
Cladoselache above is a shark that became
extinct about 225 million years ago. It
grew to 2 metres (6 feet 6 inches) in
length. Well preserved fossils have been
found around Lake Erie in the United
States. *Cladoselache* lacked an anal fin
and the fin spines were relatively flimsy
compared to those of modern sharks. The
mouth is terminal, rather than on the
underside of the head as in today's sharks.
Fossils of *Cladoselache* lack claspers and
it may be that fertilization was external.

The early record of sharks is complex
and poorly understood. Other groups came
and went after *Cladoselache*. During the
Carboniferous Period (345 to 270 million
years ago), primitive sharks known as
hybodonts ruled the seas, and provided

the basic design from which modern
sharks evolved. During the Cretaceous
Period (135 to 70 million years ago) the
hybodonts died out and were replaced by
the forerunners of modern sharks. New
adaptions included a calcified and
strengthened spinal column that improved
swimming ability, and stronger, ventrally
positioned jaws.

▶▲TAILS
The most extreme heterocercal design is
found in **thresher sharks**. The upper lobe
of the tail is elongated to equal the total
length of the shark's body. The tail had
become a weapon that the thresher uses
like a sickle. It slaps and slashes its way
through a school of fish before turning to
devour stunned and wounded victims.

In contrast, **mackerel sharks** have a
reduced upper lobe and the tail is almost
symmetrical. Caudal keels strengthen the
base of the tail so that the body is braced
against the independent beats of the
caudal fin. Mackerel sharks are among the
fastest of sharks. Two species, the
porbeagle and the **salmon shark**, have
two keels on either side of the caudal fin.

Scattered over its skin are many 'pit organs', the number and pattern varying from species to species, but being more numerous in free-swimming sharks than in the more sluggish bottom-dwelling types. These organs are basically cup-shaped, with a central hair that responds to water movements, and to pressure waves passing through the water.

Running along both sides of the shark is another sensory system called the lateral line, which is common to all fish. Its individual cells are similar in basic structure to those of the pit organs – a central hair, embedded in a gelatinous substance. But here, the individual units are linked up, to provide a more sensitive, overall picture of the surrounding ocean.

In addition to these senses that parallel our own – vision, smell and hearing – sharks have certain sensory powers which seem almost supernatural to us, because they are so alien to our own experience of the world. One is the ability to sense electricity. Dotted over the head of sharks are numerous small pores, called the ampullae of Lorenzini, after their discoverer. Recent work has shown that this sensory system is capable of detecting weak electric fields. The electric 'aura' generated by the life processes of an animal make it apparent to the shark even though it may be invisible. Thus sharks can overcome the camouflage and burying techniques which certain animals employ for defence, by sensing the electric fields that they produce. Like many animals, sharks can also detect the magnetic fields of the earth, and they may use these to navigate.

It should by now be apparent that there is a lot more to sharks than was first supposed, and that they are complex, highly evolved animals. Another exciting area of research, that is producing some surprising discoveries about sharks, has been in the field of behaviour. In the 1970s, Sonny Gruber and Arthur Myrberg did important pioneer work on bonnethead sharks *Sphyrna tiburo*, a type of small hammerhead. These were kept in a large 'semi-natural' enclosure, which the scientists watched for about 1000 man-hours. From this exhaustive study they were able to identify seventeen distinct behavioural units, eight of which were socially orientated (in other words related to the presence of another shark). Other scientists have made studies of complex shark behaviour in the wild. Don Nelson has discovered remarkable features in the behaviour of the grey reef shark *Carcharhinus amblyrhynchos*. Peter Klimley, of the Scripps Institute, has dived with scalloped hammerheads *Sphyrna lewini* and studied the interactions that occur between them as they gather in huge schools in the Sea of Cortez. This work has revealed a level of social interaction and complex behaviour that is incompatible with the traditional view of sharks – far from being primitive creatures of little intelligence, they are sophisticated social animals. But rather than report on these studies here, I will discuss them in later chapters, in the context of my own experiences with sharks.

One crucial area of shark biology remains to be described – their sexual behaviour, mating and reproduction. This too is an area where they show great specialization and advancement. Indeed, compared to the sharks and their allies, the reproductive methods of teleosts and other fish appear archaic.

The basic method of reproduction in teleost fish is called 'ovipary' – in other words, they lay eggs rather than producing live young. In most species, fertilization is external: huge numbers of eggs and sperm being released into the water together. Because of the enormous numbers involved, each egg is provided with relatively little yolk on which the developing embryo can feed. So it hatches in a small and undeveloped state, and requires a long time to reach maturity. There are several problems involved with this system. The greatest is predation: the vast majority of eggs and young are eaten by other animals long before they reach maturity – which is why so many are needed in the first place. Overall, the strategy works – the teleost fish reproduce themselves successfully. But it is a strategy that is extraordinarily wasteful in its use of raw materials.

Sharks have developed quite different strategies for reproduction. Rather than waste so much energy on masses of eggs and young, sharks concentrate their resources into producing a few young and ensuring their survival. It is the same sort of strategy that is seen in mammals and birds. Fertilization occurs within the female's body and a small number of large, well-developed young (or 'pups') are produced. These are miniature adults, capable of fending for themselves.

Internal fertilization requires some means of injecting sperm into the female's body, and sharks, like other fish, do not have a penis. Instead, male sharks have developed intromittent organs called claspers, on the underside of the pelvic fins. It is easy to distinguish a mature male shark from a female as the claspers are clearly visible in the male. During copulation the claspers point forward. Often, only one is functional, and this is inserted in the female's cloaca (the combined opening to the reproductive, urinary and digestive tracts). Mating among sharks has rarely been observed in the wild and we know very little about it. However, some small sharks in aquariums have been seen mating, for example the horn sharks *Heterodontus*. In these species the male grasps the female by a pectoral fin before inserting a clasper.

The mating habits of larger sharks are mostly unknown, but there is a strong suspicion that, in most large, predatory sharks, the male bites the female along the back and on the fins as part of the mating process. One piece of circumstantial evidence for this is that in some species the skin of the female is considerably thicker than that of the male – for instance in the blue shark *Prionace glauca*. Furthermore, it is not uncommon to see female sharks that have recent and deep bite marks on their bodies and fins.

Sharks have evolved three basic methods of development for the embryo. The most primitive is ovipary, or the laying of eggs, as in other fish. However, far fewer eggs are produced than in most teleost fish, and they are larger and better protected: a tough egg-case encapsulates the developing young, and it is filled with yolk, by which the embryo is nourished. Shark egg cases come in a variety of shapes and sizes. Those of the horn sharks are shaped like corkscrews, a shape that may have a special function: wave or current action tends to make such a structure bury itself into the sand. Other species have egg cases with long tendrils at one end so that they can become safely entangled in seaweed. These are the 'mermaid's purses' that are sometimes found on the strandline by beachcombers. Though such sharks are producing embryos that must develop outside the mother's body, they still show a considerable

How Sharks Develop

The three methods of shark development are each a considerable advance on the haphazard methods of the teleost fish. Some sharks are oviparous and lay eggs like teleosts. However, oviparous sharks lay a few, large eggs that have a good supply of yolk to nourish the developing embryo. The eggs are soft but soon harden when they come into contact with sea water. The catshark egg case shown here has tendrils that allow it to be attached to seaweeds (after Castro). Ovovivipary is the most common developmental method of sharks. The eggs hatch within the uterus of the female and are nourished by their yolk sacs. The sharpnose embryo shown here is a typical example.

Vivipary is the most advanced method of development. Viviparous sharks have a reduced yolk sac and the stalk that links it to the embryo becomes elongated and forms a placental connection with the mother's body (after Castro). Sharks evolved this method long before mammals appeared.

Catshark egg case (oviparous development)

Sharpnose shark embryo (ovoviviparous development)

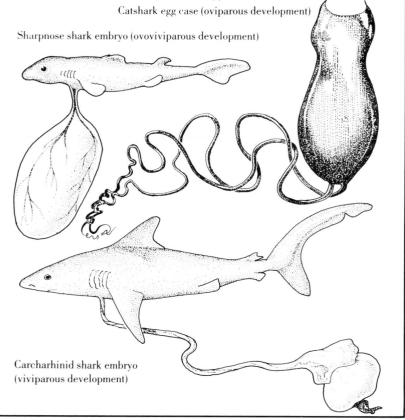

Carcharhinid shark embryo
(viviparous development)

The sharksucker *Echeneis naucrates* is one of a group of teleost fish called suckerfish or remoras, with the first dorsal fin modified into a suction pad. This is used to attach the fish to a host animal, and the sharksucker typically attaches itself to sharks. Here it feeds off ectoparasites, such as copepods, attached to the shark's skin. It also probably eats scraps from the shark's own meals. Heavily pregnant sharks often have a number of sharksuckers attached to them, and these have been observed to feed off the afterbirth when the pups are born.

advance on the ovipary of other fish, since fertilization is internal, and the young are relatively large at hatching.

The second and most common method of development for sharks is called ovovivipary (the method is less complex than the name). In this system, the eggs are kept inside the body and hatch within the mother. Each egg has a rich supply of yolk that is connected by a stalk to the embryo, and is absorbed as the embryo grows.

Some ovoviviparous species have developed a strange twist to the embryonic story – intra-uterine cannibalism. This occurs in the sand tiger *Odontaspis taurus* and various other species. Having absorbed all the yolk fairly early on, one embryo – the one that develops most quickly – goes on to feed on all the other eggs and embryos within the female. Thus only one pup survives, and most of the eggs produced serve as its nourishment. Although it seems rather gruesome, this is simply a very effective strategy for producing a single, well-developed young one: a successful evolutionary trend of which we ourselves are an example.

The third and most advanced form of development is called vivipary. In this method, once the stored yolk is absorbed by the embryo, a placental connection is established between the embryo and the mother, via an umbilical cord. This highly advanced method of development – equivalent to that found in placental mammals – is seen in some of the smooth dogfish *Mustelus*, in the requiem sharks *Carcharhinus* and the hammerheads *Sphyrna*.

Because they produce live young, ovoviviparous and viviparous sharks have far fewer offspring than other fish. Sometimes only one or two are produced, and the total number is usually less than ten, although the monkfish *Squatina squatina* produces up to twenty, and the six-gilled shark *Hexanchus griseus* gives birth to no less than forty pups. The period spent inside the mother can be very prolonged – up to 22 months in some species – and this leads to great size in the offspring. Thus the young basking shark is a full 1.5 metres (5 feet) long at birth.

There are approximately 350 species of shark known to date – only one per cent of all known fish species, but with a fascination for man that is out of all proportion to their numbers. Doubtless, as more and more of the ocean is explored, new species of shark will be found, particularly in the more remote parts of the abyssal depths. Yet those that we already know of are a diverse and extraordinary group, supremely well adapted to their way of life. Much remains to be discovered about them, but the story so far is still well worth telling.

CHAPTER THREE

SHARKS *—OF THE—* *SHALLOWS*

Long Island is situated in the middle of the Bahama chain, a long, crooked sliver of green land, dropped haphazardly in the western Atlantic, along with the 700 or so other islands that make up the Bahamas. Flying in to Long Island over the shallow tropical waters, I could see the countless reef formations that fringe the island and stretch in jagged brown lines across the sea. It was the summer of 1984, and I had come to the Bahamas in search of the sharks that live around these coral reefs. My destination was the Stella Maris Inn on Long Island, a hotel that caters for divers, and specializes in feeding sharks underwater on one of their reefs.

In the hotel bar, I tracked down the man who organizes the dives, Jason Burrows, a tall imposing Bahamian. I began asking him questions about the sharks, particularly about the species I was likely to see. To my surprise I discovered that the species he was feeding were not small inoffensive ones, like blacktips *Carcharhinus limbatus* and nurse sharks *Ginglymostoma cirratum*, as I had assumed. Instead, most of his regular diners were bull sharks *Carcharhinus leucas*, heavily built animals that favour shallow water, and are members of the group known as the requiem sharks, or, to use the scientific term, the Carcharhinids. The requiem sharks are the dominant shark predators of tropical seas, and bull sharks, which can grow to 3.4 metres (11 feet) and weigh over 200 kg (441 lb), are among the most formidable. Jason assured me that his bull sharks were considerably smaller, averaging 2 metres (6 feet 6 inches) or less in length, but I was still apprehensive. Some authorities think that the bull shark is the most dangerous shark of all for a variety of reasons. Firstly, it favours shallow, inshore tropical waters, where there tend to be people swimming. Secondly, it grows very large, and is cosmopolitan in its tastes – bull sharks eat just about anything that is edible, ranging from other sharks through to rays, all sorts of teleost fish, seabirds, turtles and a variety of mammals – dog, rat, antelope and human remains have all been found in the stomachs of bull sharks from around the world. This wide spectrum of food is made possible by the massive jaws and broad, serrated teeth of the species. To reinforce my fears, I remembered meeting spearfishermen in the Florida Keys who had been chased out of the water by aggressive bull sharks. All in all, my confidence was by then at a low ebb. But Jason went on to say that in all the years of shark-feeding at

Dawn on the flat calm shallows of a tropical lagoon in the Bahamas. Mangroves thrive at the hostile interface of sea and land. A little beyond them, a heron wades through the shallows, searching for food. As the tide comes in, particularly at dusk and during the night, so large rays and sharks enter the shallows to feed.

the Stella Maris Inn, no one had ever been bitten – however excited they became, the sharks only seemed interested in finding the dead fish on which they were fed.

So the next morning, I went with Jason to see the local sharks. We loaded our gear into the boat and set off to catch some fresh fish. The reef where the sharks are found is an isolated area of coral on the sandy bottom. Such outcrops of coral are known as patch reefs. This one is in about 10 metres (33 feet) of water, between Long Island and the neighbouring island of Little Exuma. Jason always spears his fish a couple of miles away on another 'shark-free' reef. He explained that the sharks would be quite excited enough when they caught the smell of the dead fish in the water, and that to actually spear the fish in the presence of the sharks would be foolhardy – on sensing the vibrations of the struggling fish, they would rush in without hesitation. Over the years, many other people have told me the same thing: if a shark appears when a speared fish is still struggling, the shark is unlikely to show any caution. It will charge straight in. On the other hand, if the fish is dead and the shark can only smell it, it will be more hesitant in its approach.

We arrived on a small reef and Jason prepared to spear some fish. He used a 'Hawaiian sling' – a long, steel spear with an elastic loop that can be used to shoot the spear. I gazed over the side of the boat into the water, which was amazingly clear: I could make out details in the coral about 7 metres (23 feet) below. Impatient to get into the water, I decided to snorkel while Jason was spearing fish. There was a large, squat coral head, about 10 metres (33 feet) in length, surrounded by sand. Jason swam down and speared a fish on one side, and it immediately started struggling on the spear. I happened to look over to the other side of the coral head and saw a small, pale coloured shark of about 1.25 metres (4 feet) cruising over the sand. From the high arch of its back I identified it as a small blacktip *Carcharhinus limbatus*. It had clearly sensed the struggles of the speared fish that vibrated through the water and was swimming back and forth along the coral formation, hunting for the source of the disturbance. From my vantage point I could observe the whole situation: Jason spearing fish about 5 metres (17 feet) away from a small, confused shark. Although he continued to catch fish, the shark never thought to swim around to the other side of the reef!

When Jason had caught half a dozen fish he returned to the boat and we set off for 'Shark Reef'. The dead fish were in a plastic bag, and Jason planned to feed them to the sharks one by one, by attaching each fish to a spear, about 3 metres (10 feet) in length, and holding it out. The water was breathtakingly clear, and the sandy bottom around the coral reef reflected a lot of light, making it ideal for photography. Almost immediately two sharks appeared. One was fat and heavily pregnant, about 1.5 metres (5 feet) in length. It was another blacktip. Then a sleeker, more streamlined shark glided into view, a Caribbean reef shark *Carcharhinus perezi*. Jason took a fish out of the bag and impaled it on the end of the spear, holding it out over the sand. When the sharks smelled the fish, they started swimming faster, back and forth, keeping their distance. They were quite cautious, sometimes swimming off for a minute before reappearing. I checked the controls on my camera and waited. Minutes passed. The sharks came and went, but would not grab the

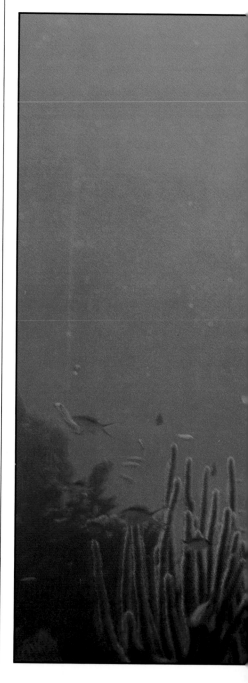

A bull shark powers its way across the reef searching for the source of the dead fish smell. This angle shows the characteristic heavy-headed shape of the species. Remarkably, the bull shark is not confined to sea water and will penetrate freshwater rivers and enters inland lakes throughout the tropics.

fish. Then a bull shark appeared. My first impression was of something much heavier, blunt and strong, its front half almost deformed by its thick-set strength. But it was as cautious as the other sharks, staying too far off for a good picture. After about fifteen minutes another reef shark appeared. This one did not hesitate, but came straight in at speed to grab the proffered fish. It caught me by surprise and although I quickly photographed the fleeing shape, I knew that I had missed the moment. Jason put another fish on the spear and I looked out for the bull shark. But it was the blacktip that flashed in to grab the fish. We carried on waiting, another fish on display. The sharks, however, had had enough and did not come back. So Jason emptied the bag of fish, and we returned to the boat.

I had to admit to being disappointed. The bull shark had shown

little interest, and the smaller sharks were timid. But Jason assured me that it was an unusually quiet feed and promised me more action the next day. He was right. When we returned the next day with fresh fish we immediately spotted the dark, broad shape of a bull shark moving across the sand below. Then another. We descended to our position, and already the sharks were there. Three good-sized bull sharks and a smaller Caribbean reef shark. Jason put the bag of fish on the sand and I took up position next to it, watching the bull sharks out on the sand. Compared to the reef shark, they looked ugly and blunt. I fired my camera to test that it was working. The strobe flashed and emitted its loud, high-pitched whine as it recharged. I crouched down next to Jason's bag of fish, to try to be in the optimum position when the sharks came in.

What I had failed to notice, absorbed as I was in the business of

The Caribbean reef shark lacks the heavyweight build of the bull shark and is more elegantly proportioned. The species is confined to the warmer, inshore waters of the western Atlantic. It can grow to 3 metres (10 feet) and is a powerful hunter in the clear, reef areas that it prefers.

photography, was the state of the fish bag. It was open, and the blood and oil of the speared fish was seeping slowly out, covering me with its insidious smell. I realized too late what had happened. Suddenly the sharks started coming in – but not for the fish – it was me that they were investigating. One after another they came barreling in from the sand, swerving off at the last moment. I looked over to Jason and saw that he had sensibly retreated into the coral. But, since I smelled of dead fish, following suit would not be much help – to a shark I was as conspicuous as a red flashing light. I realized that there was not much I could do, so I held my ground, waiting for each shark to come in. On several occasions I had to beat my fins on the head of a shark, to make it turn off. But, despite my alarm, I did not get the impression that they were doing anything more than looking for the fish. As they swept past, I could hear a thudding sound –

whether it was the noise of their tails pumping against the water, or was generated from within their bodies I do not know. The sharks were now moving all over the place, up through the coral and in from behind. A bull shark approached from the sand and I took a picture of it. I heard the reassuring whine of the strobe as it recharged and then there was a thud and the camera was jolted half out of my hands. A pale belly shot past my head from behind. One of the sharks had bitten the strobe. . . . By now the situation was out of hand and I retreated up into the coral. The sharks made a few more bold passes at me but then withdrew to the sand below. After a few minutes, things calmed down, and we returned to the boat.

Back on board, Jason apologized for having left the bag open, but I knew it was my own fault – I should not have positioned myself next

Right and below
Heavy-set and powerful bull sharks appear before me. Attracted by the blood and oil seeping out from the fish bag, they come closer and closer, growing in confidence. Growing to over 3 metres (10 feet) and feeding on a wide range of prey, bull sharks are large and voracious predators and considered dangerous to humans.

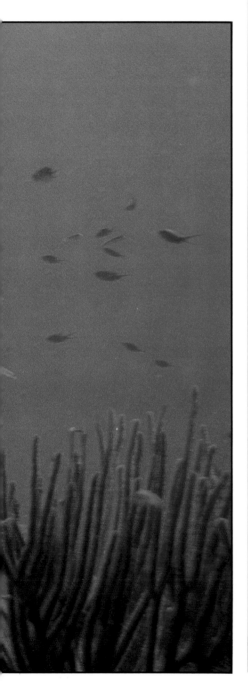

to it. I reflected on the shark that bit my strobe – or rather, the fact that it bit it as it was recharging and emitting its high-pitched whine. Considering that the strobe was silent for most of the dive, I wondered if the shark was attracted to it by the whining noise. Whatever the reason for the attack, I knew that it had been a potentially dangerous situation. I had been incautious and would have to take more care in the future.

SOUTH BIMINI, THE BAHAMAS

I was pleased with my shots of the bull sharks, but I knew there were many other species of shark common in the shallow waters of the Bahamas and the Florida coast. Unfortunately, I did not know how to locate them. One could spend weeks and weeks taking dead fish down on various reefs, hoping that a certain species of shark would turn up – in all likelihood it would amount to a huge waste of time. In fact I tried this method, later in the year, off Andros Island, and saw only one small Caribbean reef shark. It was not until January of 1986 that I made any real progress photographing sharks in this part of the world. In December of 1985 I wrote to Sonny Gruber at Miami University and explained to him that I was interested in photographing sharks. I knew that he led scientific expeditions to the waters of Bimini in the Bahamas to study sharks. In my letter I listed those sharks that I hoped to photograph in these waters, including the tiger shark *Galeocerdo cuvieri* and the lemon shark *Negaprion brevirostris*. Sonny wrote back to say that he could guarantee that I would get pictures of these species, and of several other sharks as well. However, the next expedition was leaving almost immediately, in mid-January, so I would have to act promptly if I wanted to make the trip. I assembled my gear and headed for Miami, where the scientists who were going on the expedition were gathering. They would be working from a research vessel, the *Cape Florida*, and I was assigned two people who would work with me. Jeff Tatelman, Sonny's assistant, would operate the boat we would be using, and Mike Braun would help me underwater with the sharks.

When everyone was assembled and all the final arrangements had been made, the *Cape Florida* set sail from Miami for Bimini. Bimini is located about 90 km (59 miles) due east of Miami, across the waters of the Gulf Stream. Actually, there are two islands, North Bimini and South Bimini. North Bimini is the more built up of the two, and better known to tourists. Ernest Hemingway lived here, and the rich fishing of the Gulf Stream was the inspiration for many of his stories. South Bimini is a few hundred metres away, connected to North Bimini by a shallow, sandy bay.

These tiny islands lie 440 km (270 miles) northwest of Long Island, at the far end of the Bahama chain, and their coasts and surrounding waters are quite different in nature. Here there are no fringing reefs, yet the coastline is equally fascinating, a complex of lagoons and mangrove swamps that makes the dividing line between land and sea difficult to pinpoint.

Mangroves are a group of trees and shrubs that have adapted to life in the extremely hostile conditions of tidal areas: they must survive not only being exposed at low tide, but also having their roots swamped in salty water at high tide. Their success is the basis of a complex ecosystem because the mangroves act as anchors, holding back sediment with their root systems to create the swamp below. As a mangrove colony grows and becomes better established, so all sorts of animals move in – both above and below the water line. The decay of mangrove leaves is hastened by fungi and bacteria, and they become an important nutrient for animals to feed on.

Snorkel in the murky waters of a mangrove system and you will see

An immature nurse shark *Ginglymostoma cirratum* rests on the bottom in a murky tidal creek in the Florida Keys. Here it can hunt for crabs and worms among the algal-covered rocks that surround it. It is also relatively safe from large predatory sharks that enter its drab world at night.

numerous crabs, snails, jellyfish and small fish. On a filling tide, schools of fish will come in to feed, retreating later as the tide ebbs. These fluctuations in activity can be dramatic. My first experience of mango swamps was in the Florida Keys, only a short boat-ride southwest of Bimini. The Florida coastline at this point is a complex series of creeks, channels and lagoons formed by the anchoring and reclaiming action of mangroves. Large mangrove islands, on which many other plants and animals have become established, separate inner reaches of water – called 'sounds' – from the open sea. The two are linked by channels, usually less than 50 metres (55 yards) in width, through which the tide rushes. My brother Nicholas has spent many hours fishing these channels and has built up a fascinating picture of the populations of animals that come and go with the tide. During the day the creeks are all but deserted. If you put a bait down during daylight hours then you would be unlikely to catch anything.

Right and below right
Animals that live in exposed areas of sand have developed many means of defence. The demon stinger *Inimicus sp.* demonstrates several. It can bury itself in the sand, with just it eyes and mouth exposed. Here, it is all but invisible to predators as it waits in ambush for crabs and small fish to come too close. When removed from the sand, it erects its venomous dorsal spines which can cause agonizing wounds to anyone unfortunate enough to step on it.

But at night, when the tide is just beginning to flow back out to sea, it is a very different story. For about half an hour the tarpon come through, swimming in great numbers back to sea. You can tell that they are tarpon even without catching them, because of the characteristic gulping noise they make on the surface. Just as the numbers of tarpon are thinning out, sharks come through – lemon sharks, nurse sharks, blacktips and bonnetheads, all about 1.5 metres (5 feet) in length. Then, after half an hour of frantic activity, all goes quiet again.

The sharks are not always there: on some nights there are none. On others, when the conditions seem the same, the channels are thick with sharks. Perhaps they do not come in every night – or perhaps they swim back to sea through other channels. Whatever the explanation, they tend to be there in great numbers or not at all. It is known that most sharks feed at night. Presumably they, and the tarpon, are following schools of prey fish that come and go with the ebb and flow of the tide.

In the Bimini lagoon there is the same sort of pattern, with a nightly influx of sharks and other predatory fish in search of food. But that is only part of its attraction for Sonny Gruber. As he explained to me on board the *Cape Florida*:

'The beauty of the Bimini lagoon is that we have the complete lifecycle of a large shark here. In the early summer, pregnant female lemon sharks come into the mangrove shallows to drop their young. So we can study the juveniles as they grow up in the shallows. Here they are relatively safe from predators, though adult lemon sharks do feed on pups. When they reach about one-and-a-half metres the juveniles move into deeper water. At night, the adults come in over the shallow sands to feed. It all adds up to a fairly comprehensive picture of the lemon shark's lifecycle.'

Part of Sonny's research project involves recording the daily and seasonal movements of lemon sharks, by capturing them, fitting them with radio-transmitters, and then releasing them again. The sharks are tracked by listening in to their transmitters, each of which has its own characteristic signal. Eventually, the whole area around Bimini will have monitors positioned across the bottom. When the lemon sharks are released into the lagoon, their positions will be automatically and continuously recorded by the monitors. This information will then be passed into a computer for analysis. The beauty of this system is that the operation should work automatically for many months, providing detailed information on the movements of the sharks. Another experiment that is underway is the measuring of the heart rate of captured sharks by surgically implanted electrodes and electro-cardiogram apparatus. This is to gain better knowledge of their metabolic rates.

In order to catch the sharks, baited hooks are set in the shallows behind South Bimini. These hooks are attached, by wire traces, to a central long line running along the bottom. The hooks are baited just before dusk, and the next morning the lines are inspected to see what sharks have been caught. Then the sharks are carefully removed from the line, taken on board the *Cape Florida*, measured and fitted with transmitters. Before being released, they are also injected with tetracycline, which does them no harm, but stains their backbones. As a shark grows, rings form in the backbone and these can be monitored by the staining technique. At a later date, if the shark is caught, examination of the backbone will reveal the tetracycline stain. By referring to the data from its previous capture, Sonny can obtain valuable information about the growth-rate and age of the shark. Finally, samples of blood are taken from the sharks. These are put into a centrifuge to separate the serum from the blood cells. The serum is being used in an attempt to find a cure for AIDS, thanks to a remarkable property of shark blood. Higher vertebrates have evolved complex and specialized antibodies which are highly effective in some ways, but are not always able to combat new diseases. In contrast, sharks produce more generalized antibodies that can act against a wider range of diseases. Sharks are also of interest to cancer researchers, because unlike other fish, they do not get cancer. It is possible that this interesting feature of shark biology may one day greatly benefit humans.

Inevitably, species other than lemon sharks are caught, and some sharks die on the baited lines, but their deaths are not in vain. Their livers and muscles are analysed for metal content – twenty-seven different metals are looked at, in an attempt to monitor marine pollution by industrial wastes. Skin samples are analysed for dermal denticle morphology. Stomach contents are inspected to build up a picture of the shark's diet, while taxonomists measure every part of each shark's body and preserve the jaws. Experiments are also being done on the hormonal secretions in sharks, to further our knowledge of their reproductive and developmental systems. The placental relationship between viviparous sharks and their pups, with its intriguing parallels to our own form of reproduction, is being studied in detail.

No-one could be more committed to preserving sharks than Sonny Gruber, and, as he explained to me, he feels that the sharks killed each season for these experiments are entirely justified:

'The few sharks that we take here are necessary for understanding the dynamics of the local population. From the information gathered here we are better able to protect the species as a whole.'

'We are trying to understand sharks as an integral part of the ecosystem so that they can be better protected from over-fishing and even extermination. Several other shark species are near to extinction thanks to over-fishing – the soupfin shark of the Pacific, the porbeagle of the North Atlantic and the Cuban night shark of the tropical western Atlantic, for example.'

'We have learned from tests on lemon sharks in aquaria that they do not eat as much or feed as often as one might think. A lemon shark loses about one per cent of its body weight per day and can last up to twenty days without feeding. Typically, lemon sharks only feed every third or fourth day. When they do feed, they don't eat a lot: perhaps five per cent of their body weight. Given this knowledge, it is not surprising that a lemon shark can take from fifteen to twenty years to reach sexual maturity. We are gradually putting the whole picture together and assessing the impact of huge-scale commercial fishing on shark populations. The results are very disturbing. Mature sharks are few and far between, and often decades old. They simply cannot sustain the heavy pressures of commercial fishing, or even in many cases, the concentrated effects of local sport fishing.'

A few hours after setting sail from Miami, we arrived off South

Bimini, and the *Cape Florida* dropped anchor. That evening, the ship was in a state of barely concealed chaos, with scientists from as far afield as Japan setting up equipment in preparation for their experiments. When finally everything was sorted out, Mike Braun came over and talked to me:

'We'll definitely get lemon sharks, maybe as big as two-and-a-half metres. Tigers too; I've had them over four metres on the long line. Maybe a bull shark – they get big too, but this is not the best time of year for them. And we should get blacktips, nurse sharks and a couple of smaller species – sharpnose and blacknose. We're going to put a long line down in deeper water as well, at about thirty metres, so we may get a great hammerhead. I'll help you with the sharks underwater. When we find one that you want to photograph, I'll get it off the line and revive it for you.'

Early next morning a report came in that there was a 2.5-metre (8-foot) lemon shark on one of the lines, and Jeff Tatelman and I set off for the position. We sped over to the far side of South Bimini in his boat and came to a halt in the shallows, next to the scientists who had found the shark. Mike was elsewhere, checking other lines and came in on the radio:

'Jeremy. Watch out for the lemon shark when you get near it. Tigers are O.K. on the end of the line, but lemons will try to bite.' I noted his advice, and Sonny came on the radio to repeat the warning. I took a pole down with me when I got in, to fend off the shark, should I have to.

A nasty moment as this captured lemon shark lunges at me. It is constrained by the line on which it has been caught but I hold my metal pole ready to fend it off if necessary. Abundant on both sides of the Americas, this species prefers inshore, tropical waters. Lemon sharks can be found in very shallow water (nursery grounds for the pups), and they can also penetrate fresh water, though not to the same extent as the bull shark.

The water was not as clear as I had hoped: perhaps 3 metres (10 feet) of visibility at most. I could see the large mass of the shark lying on the bottom. It was gulping water in through its mouth for respiration. Each time it opened its mouth, I noticed an impressive display of teeth. The shark was a pale yellow-brown colour, though not quite 'lemon' yellow, and heavy-bodied – I guessed it weighed over 100 kg (220 lb). A wicked-looking animal. It lifted off the bottom and tried to swim away from me, but it could only go a short distance before the line restricted it and it sank to the bottom. I took up position in front of it, keeping the pole ready to push the shark away should I have to. Even as I took a picture it snapped at me, trying to reach me, before it sank back to the bottom. I took some more shots and then returned to the boat. Jeff asked me if I wanted to wait and photograph the shark when it was released, after being measured and tagged. I looked at the murky water and realized that I would have to be very close to it to get a picture. Given its aggressive nature, I decided against it.

The next day started with the news I had been waiting for. A 2.5-metre (8-foot) tiger shark was on one of the shallow lines, in good condition. Tiger sharks are among the most impressive of tropical sharks. So-called because of the tiger-like stripes on the sides of the body, the name applies equally well to their predatory status. The stripes actually fade on large individuals – and tiger sharks get very large indeed. There are occasional reports of tiger sharks of over 5 metres (17 feet) in length and other, unconfirmed reports of tiger sharks considerably larger still. As with many other species of shark, the females grow much larger than the males. Tiger sharks are known man-eaters, and have many features in common with other dangerous sharks such as the bull shark: a huge mouth, serrated teeth, and a very broad diet. In fact tiger sharks will eat just about anything: all sorts of fish, including other sharks and rays, marine mammals, octopuses and squid, lobsters, crabs, shellfish, even jellyfish. Tiger sharks are found worldwide in the tropics and in the Pacific they even eat sea snakes. They also take terrestrial carrion – dead pigs, dogs and cattle – and will swallow many inedible things, including wood and metal. In many parts of the world, tiger sharks are greatly feared. Luckily they tend to have a feeding pattern that minimizes their contact with humans: during the day they stay in deep water, venturing into the shallows only at night. Large tiger sharks doubtless cruise off tourist beaches during the night.

I talked to Mike and we decided on a plan of action. Enough tiger sharks had already been caught for research purposes, so this one was to be released, and, with luck, photographed at the same time. Mike told me that however dangerous tiger sharks are under normal circumstances, once they have been hooked and tired on the line, they are almost docile. So we decided to take it to a channel that was about 30 metres (33 yards) wide, with quite shallow, clear water. Mike would release the shark towards me, and because the water was shallow, and the channel relatively narrow, the shark should swim towards me and not go off in another direction. Mike also explained that tiger sharks go into a kind of shocked state if you touch their backs. As soon as a tiger shark feels pressure on its back, it will stop swimming and sink to the bottom. This gave me a means of stopping the shark if it should try to swim past me before I'd finished shooting

Above
Like bull sharks, tiger sharks are known man-eaters. They also have a huge mouth, with serrated teeth and a very broad diet. They have been observed in shallow water gouging troughs in the sand as they search for hidden lobsters, crabs and rays.

Left
Released in the channel, the Bimini tiger shark quickly revives. With each bend of its tail the shark moves a little faster, and gulping mouthfuls of water, it awakens from its docile trance.

– all I had to do was grab its back and it would sink like a stone. Jeff, Mike and I eventually managed to lift the heavy shark into the boat and quieten it down. Mike draped a wet towel over its head and it lay quite still. Then we rushed over to the channel as we had planned. On first being returned to the water, the shark sank and for a terrible moment I thought it was dead, but Mike jumped in and started walking it around, pushing it gently to force water through its gills. Slowly, it began to revive. I followed him in and took up position in the channel. Then Mike released the shark. It swam towards me much faster than I expected – it had recovered remarkably fast from its ordeal. I took as many shots as I could, and as it swam past me, I followed Mike's instructions, grabbing its back and hanging on to the dorsal fin. To my surprise the technique worked like magic. The shark immediately stopped swimming and sank to the bottom, as immobile as a kitten held by the scruff of the neck.

Before it could set off again, Mike got hold of it, while I moved further along the channel and set up my camera once more. Then we repeated the procedure. After a couple more tries we were getting

Right above
The Caribbean sharpnose shark is a small shark of the Caribbean, Bahamas and warmer Atlantic waters of South America. The tails of the two pups can be seen emerging from the cloaca of this female. Though closely related to the genus *Carcharhinus*, whose members are viviparous, sharpnose sharks are ovoviviparous; the developing pups gain nourishment from their large yolk sacs. Unlike viviparous sharks, there is no placental connection to the mother.

Right
A 2.5-metre (8-foot) nurse shark caught on the Bimini long line. Nurse sharks normally spend the day at rest hidden in crevices on the bottom and use the hours of darkness to forage for food.

Another Bimini long line shark, this time an elegantly proportioned blacktip shark *Carcharhinus limbatus*. This is a requiem shark with a long snout and high back and characteristic black tips to the fins.

quite expert at it, but each time the shark revived a little more and swam a little faster. Clearly it was coming out of its shocked state, and might soon become dangerous. On the next pass, it swam past me at even greater speed, its strength returning. I decided not to grab it this time and watched as it swam on out of the channel, blending into the deep yellow haze of the sandy lagoon. During the following days more sharks were caught. A pregnant sharpnose shark *Rhizoprionodon porosus* was captured as she was about to give birth, with the tails of two pups emerging from her cloaca. When I reached the site, Guido Dingerkus, one of the scientists on the trip, was pushing her through the water to keep her alive so that I could get a photograph. Other sharpnose sharks were caught, and several blacknose sharks *Carcharhinus acronotus*, but sadly they were all dead by the morning. And every day I hoped to hear that a great hammerhead had been captured on the deepwater longline. Two days

One afternoon, while I was snorkelling off Bimini, a group of spotted eagle rays *Aetobatus narinari* swam by, one (foreground) displaying the unmistakable wound of a shark bite in its pectoral wingtip. Despite the barbed, venomous spine carried in the base of the tail, eagle rays are a favourite meal of several large tropical shark species.

The dark marking on the end of the snout gives the blacknose shark its name. Found in the warmer inshore waters of the western Atlantic, this is one of the smaller sharks of the *Carcharhinus* genus. Most adults are little over a metre (3 feet) in length and preyed upon by larger sharks.

Left
The great hammerhead *Sphyrna mokarran* from the long line. This is the largest, the most powerful and the most aggresive of the hammerhead sharks. It is distributed worldwide in tropical seas and feeds on a broad range of prey, though rays are a favourite meal. Great hammerheads are thought to be nomadic, ranging into shallow water and also far out into the ocean.

Below
A 2.75-metre (9-foot) bignose shark *Carcharhinus altimus* slips back into the depths. The bignose shark is a large, powerful requiem shark that hunts along the deepwater edges of the tropical con-

tinental shelf. This individual was caught by a fisherman on the bottom in 200 metres (650 feet) of water off Miami, Florida. It was brought to the surface and photographed as it was released.

Overleaf
The seascape in the shallow waters of temperate seas is rich in seaweeds and none is more spectacular than the Californian giant kelp. This magnificent plant forms great forests within which countless animals live. Here, a school of jack mackerel *Trachurus symmetricus* have massed within the sheltering arches of the kelp.

before the end of the trip a morning radio call announced just that, so we rushed to the deepwater line to photograph the shark, praying that it would still be alive. But when we got there the animal was dead. By the end of the field trip I was more than satisfied – I had photographed seven species of shark in those waters. But if only the hammerhead had lived! I did not know then that I was soon to see a vast school of hammerheads, in the Red Sea (see Chapter Four).

——— CATALINA ISLAND, CALIFORNIA ———

Moving northwards from the warm waters of the Bahamas brings new groups of sharks into ascendancy, others into decline. Since sharks are basically cold blooded, their metabolic rates are largely under the control of the environment, though a few species, as already mentioned, can maintain a body

temperature significantly above that of the surrounding water. As we move north and the temperature of the water falls, so certain species become established while others thin out and vanish. Not only does the temperature of the water directly affect the sharks' metabolic rates, but it has secondary effects which also influence their distribution. One is that the solubility of gases varies according to water temperature, and this affects animal life because the amount of oxygen dissolved in the sea water is crucial to their respiratory requirements. Oxygen is significantly less soluble in warmer water: in shallow, tropical lagoons I have seen oxygen (produced by all plants during photosynthesis) bubbling up from algae on the bottom. In cold water this would not happen — the oxygen would dissolve as it was produced.

There are other factors that affect the distribution of sharks. The clarity of the water, the depth of penetration of light, oceanic currents and the availability of prey animals — all these interact to determine where a particular species is found.

Some species of shark that have a limited tolerance for temperature change will migrate seasonally north or south, to remain within their preferred range, while others, although more tolerant of temperature fluctuations, will migrate in pursuit of prey. Consequently, there is no clear dividing line between the shark species found in tropical and temperate waters. Some species are plentiful in both, the shortfin mako *Isurus oxyrinchus* for example, which is widespread throughout the tropical, sub-tropical and temperate waters of the world, being able to handle a wide range of temperatures. On the other hand, though the blue shark *Prionace glauca* prefers a cool environment, it is abundant not only in temperate waters, but also in the tropics. Here it performs what is known as 'tropical submergence' — spending most of the time in deeper waters, to attain its preferred temperature.

The mean average surface temperature of the ocean off California (north of Baja) is between 10°C and 20°C (50°F and 68°F). This is termed a temperate, or warm-temperate range (to distinguish it from the cool-temperate or boreal range, of 5°C to 10°C – 41°F to 50°F – to the north of it.) The water temperature here contrasts with that in the tropical region (which includes Florida and the Bahamas, although they are north of the tropic of Cancer) where the mean surface temperature of the seawater is greater than 20°C (68°F). Off the Californian coast the water feels cold even when the sun is shining. Yet California's coastline has its own special attraction for divers, a unique habitat known as 'kelp forest'.

The backbone of the kelp forest is the giant kelp *Macrocystis pyrifera*. Individual plants can climb to the surface from a depth of 30 metres (100 feet) to bask their broad fronds on the surface in green canopies. A healthy kelp forest can cover several square kilometres, but kelp forests are comparatively rare, for they need a special set of environmental conditions. A rocky bottom on which the plants can anchor themselves is essential, plus a strong current to provide the plants with a rich supply of nutrients. Once established, the kelp forest is a valuable habitat for other species. Hundreds of different animals and plants, including other seaweeds, worms, molluscs, crabs, starfish and a great variety of fish, have adapted themselves to shelter in this rich green world.

In August 1986 I was fortunate enough to be able to join Don Nelson and several of his research students on his boat off Catalina Island, which is 30 kilometres (19 miles) from the coast of California. Don is a biology professor at California State University, Long Beach. His speciality is sharks and his passion is their study, not in a laboratory, but in the wild.

One of Don's students, Rocky Strong, is studying the Californian horn shark *Heterodontus francisci*, a curious-looking shark that is common in the shallow waters around Catalina Island. During that trip Rocky agreed to take me down on a dive and show me some horn sharks so that I could photograph them, and then — if we had enough air and enough bottom-time left — to go deeper in search of an angel shark *Squatina californica*.

This is a juvenile leopard shark of about 70 cm (just over 2 feet) in length. Adults do not normally exceed 1.6 metres (5 feet) and their colour fades to a dull brown. Leopard sharks are well able to rest on the bottom, where they are effectively camouflaged.

I had already photographed two other sharks common in these waters – a leopard shark *Triakis semifasciata* and a swell shark *Cephaloscyllium ventriosum*. Both are interesting for several reasons, but neither of them was my reason for coming to Catalina Island. For while the leopard shark and swell shark are both fairly typical-looking sharks, the angel shark and the horn shark represent more extreme modifications of the basic shark design. The prospect of photographing both on one dive was exciting indeed.

Kitted up in our diving equipment, we set off for the buoy where the dive would begin. There was a current working against us, and it was taking Rocky and I longer than we had expected to swim to the buoy. Indeed, though it was a mere 30 metres (33 yards) ahead, we were making very slow progress. I was carrying two bulky underwater cameras which made me even slower than Rocky, and he was gradually pulling ahead of me. I envied him his dry suit – in my wet suit I could feel the coolness of the surface water and knew that it would be much colder below. It was many years since I had dived in anything but tropical waters and I was unaccustomed to the cold.

Ten murky metres (33 feet) below me I could just make out the bottom – sand and scattered masses of seaweed. It reminded me of dives, many years ago, off the south coast of England. Beneath me, something dark caught my attention as it moved across the sand. The body was flattened and shaped like a kite, but with a long, strong, shark-like tail. I realized that it was a type of ray called a guitarfish, an animal that looks half-shark and half-ray. I would have loved to have dived down and photographed it, but in that current I could not have reached it. By the time I had got down to the bottom it would have gone. And so would Rocky. So I ignored the temptation.

Eventually we reached the buoy and grabbed hold of it for a short rest. Thirty minutes of swimming to cover 30 metres (33 yards)! Then we set our watches and descended, gripping the thick, barnacled

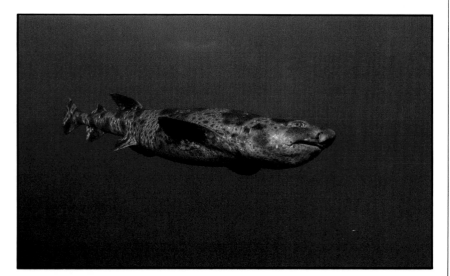

above and right
The swell shark's technique of filling its stomach with water or air to greatly increase its size is useful defensive behaviour. For example, an alarmed shark can swallow water and so inflate itself in a rock crevice from which it cannot be removed. A sluggish swimmer, the swell shark hunts at night sucking up fish that are asleep on the bottom. The enormous mouth can also be used to trick an unfortunate fish: the shark holds its mouth open and the fish swims in, by mistake.

chain of the buoy to offset the sideways drag of the current. Every metre that we descended, the current lessened, but it also grew colder. At 18 metres (59 feet) we reached the bottom–rock and sand, covered in dark green fronds of kelp.

To the right I could see that the bottom dropped sharply to much deeper water. Rocky began looking for the horn sharks, which spend the hours of daylight hidden under seaweed and in rock crevices. He lifted several broad fronds of kelp and looked beneath them. Within less than a minute he found a small horn shark, resting in the shade of a kelp frond. It was a juvenile, about 40 centimetres (16 inches) long and, unlike the adults, covered in brown spots. He gestured at me to take a picture of it – but there was a problem. In lifting up the fronds of kelp, we had disturbed the sand and the water was too murky. I took a couple of shots – just in case this was the only horn shark I ever saw – and then gestured that I had finished. Rocky picked up the small shark and put it into a bag, to be tagged, measured, weighed and released. We kept searching and found another, larger horn shark of over a metre (3 feet) in length. But again the act of searching had stirred up the water around the shark too much for a good photograph. I attempted to communicate this to Rocky, and I signalled downwards: we were obviously going to need another method to photograph the horn sharks, so I thought we might as well go straight after the angel sharks now. We headed off down the rock and seaweed slope, and suddenly the cold water got even colder as we passed through what is known as the thermocline – a meeting point between two blocks of water of markedly different temperatures and densities. Because of the temperature change the animals living above the thermocline are often very different to those living below it.

The water was now unpleasantly cold – I would guess 14°C (57°F) at the most. We continued down to 32 metres (105 feet) where the slope suddenly gave way to a sandy bottom in a murky green world. Rocky swam off, staring at the bottom, paying particular attention to the areas where the sand met the kelp-covered slope above. He stopped and pointed beneath me. I peered down – nothing to see but sand and a few grey pebbles. He carried on pointing, so I looked a little closer. Then I realized that the pebbles were not pebbles at all, but splotches of colour on something half-buried in the sand. I could make out a tail, and, more or less, a head. It was an angel shark of about 1.5 metres (5 feet) in length. But before I could photograph it I knew I would have to remove the sand so that it was visible. Its camouflage was too good to make a comprehensible photograph. I carefully wafted my hand back and forth above the shark in an attempt to remove the sand layer that it was hiding under. It put up with this for only a short while before erupting from the sand with a lazy shrug, and swimming off into the depths.

We were out of bottom-time and low on air, so Rocky and I returned to the surface, letting the current carry us back to Don Nelson's anchored research vessel, the *Discovery*. While Rocky was busy measuring, weighing and tagging the two horn sharks he had caught, I discussed with Don the problems to be overcome in order to photograph these two types of shark. He suggested that, later in the day, I should dive off a small rocky island called Ship Rock which we could see jutting out of the sea about a mile from our anchorage. Don explained that the water there is often relatively clear and also that the marine life around the rock is spectacular. The giant kelp *Macrocystis pyrifera* forms green cloisters and arches through which schools of fish swarm. Horn sharks are well hidden in the crevices and difficult to find, but angel sharks are plentiful on the sand in the deeper water.

That afternoon, I prepared to dive on Ship Rock, with another of Don's students, Larry Smith. Larry is studying chemical shark repellency – what chemicals can repel sharks and therefore, perhaps, prevent shark attacks. When we arrived at Ship Rock, I could see the thick green fronds of kelp forming a layer on the surface. A couple of sea lions splashed through the kelp as we rolled into the water, and at once I could see that it was clearer than before. Larry headed down towards the bottom and I followed, passing numerous fish that I half-recognized as cousins of tropical species. At 10 metres (33 feet), we reached the rocks below, billowing with countless varieties of seaweed, every one a different shape, and a different shade of green or brown. The richness of these waters was stunning. Bright orange fish, called garibaldi fish, flitted all over the rocks, together with many other, less conspicuous species. We descended the rocky slope, moving through gaps in the great climbing columns of the kelp forest. I glanced back up to the surface and was reminded of the fairy tale of Jack-and-the-Beanstalk. At 25 metres (82 feet) Larry and I passed through the same cruel thermocline into a darker, duller world. At 33 metres (110 feet) we reached the end of the rocks and the beginnings of the sand.

There were angel sharks everywhere – on the sand, some buried, some exposed, all stationary. I swam 10 metres (11 yards) and counted twelve sharks lying around. When I moved a little deeper, however, the numbers quickly declined. Perhaps they mass at the edge of the kelp to ambush any fish that strays from the shelter of the weeds and rocks. I picked out one to photograph, and he remained motionless, seemingly oblivious to my presence.

Don later told me that a colleague of his had estimated the number of angel sharks around Catalina Island to be about 4,000 – an

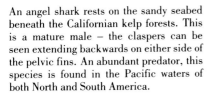

An angel shark rests on the sandy seabed beneath the Californian kelp forests. This is a mature male – the claspers can be seen extending backwards on either side of the pelvic fins. An abundant predator, this species is found in the Pacific waters of both North and South America.

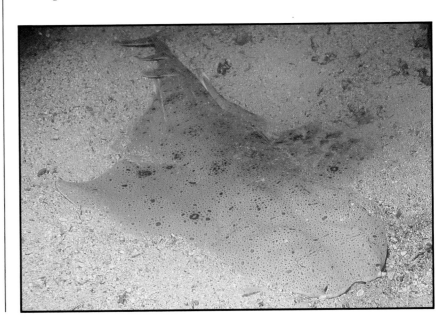

astonishing number for such a small area. I asked him how this number was arrived at, and he explained the procedure: imagine that you have a jar filled with rice and you want to know roughly how many grains there are in the jar, but cannot count them all up. Instead, you remove a known number of grains (say 100) and then label them with a dab of paint. You put them back into the jar and shake it thoroughly so that they are mixed in with all the others. Now, you remove a sample of rice grains from the jar – again, a hundred. In that number you find ten of the grains you marked. You know that you marked a hundred, and that the ratio of the marked-to-unmarked is one-to-ten. Therefore, there must be approximately ten times as many grains in the jar as the number you marked, in other words, about a thousand. In the same way, you catch and tag a known number of angel sharks, or any other animal. You then return them to the sea and let them mix in with the rest of the population. At a later date, you observe the number of tagged versus untagged. From this ratio, you can get a rough idea of the total population. It is known as the mark-release-recapture method.

Now that the angel sharks had been photographed, only the horn sharks remained. Rocky explained that they are nocturnal, coming out of their daytime retreats at nightfall, to clamber across the rocks on their broad pectoral fins, searching for sea urchins. They can be found in water as shallow as 10 metres (33 feet) when feeding. Rocky's research is involved with the movement of horn sharks, and he has fitted radio-transmitters to several of them. By hunting around in a boat and dipping a hydrophone into the water, it is possible for

The Californian horn shark uses its strong pectoral fins to clamber over the rocks in search of sea urchins. Its teeth are fused into a cobbled pavement-like structure, ideal for crushing and breaking up its food. Note the exposed fin spines on both dorsal fins. This is a mature specimen about 1 metre (3 feet) in length.

him to locate, identify and follow each 'tagged' shark.

I had little difficulty in persuading him to take me down on his dive that night, and a few hours later we were moving across the darkened waters of the bay, tracking down the signals from a shark. Sure enough we were led to a shallow rock reef and when we dived down on it, we were not surprised to find hundreds of sea urchins, the horn shark's favourite meal. Dispersed among them were horn sharks, some resting, some swimming. In fact, as I swam down the anchor chain, the first horn shark I saw was swimming frantically around the anchor. It looked as if the anchor had landed near him and scared him out of his wits. Eventually he calmed down, and I set to work. Now that they were out in the open, photographing the horn sharks was a great deal easier than it had been on my first abortive dive. The only problem that I had to contend with was how to photograph them without impaling myself on their food supply – the sea urchins.

─────── SOUTH PACIFIC CORAL REEFS ───────

Kelp forests, like mangrove swamps, are an important type of shallow-water habitat, invaluable to sharks, as to many other forms of life. Of all the shallow-water environments though, none is richer or more intricate than that of the coral reef. A wide range of shark species, some similar, some distinct, have adapted to assume a great range of predatory lifestyles within this marine ecosystem.

Some species of shark visit coral reefs often, others only occasionally. Still others have adapted specifically to thrive on coral reefs. All of the species of tropical sharks that I have mentioned so far can be found on coral reefs, as well as in other shallow-water habitats. Some – such as the bull and tiger shark – are distributed worldwide in tropical waters. Others, such as the Caribbean reef shark and the blacknose shark, have limited ranges, both being from the warmer inshore waters of the western Atlantic.

Coral reefs are found only in a certain, restricted range of conditions, for corals are fussy creatures. They demand shallow seas where the temperature does not fall below 20°C (68°F) and where the water is relatively clear, since sediment deposited on coral will kill it. The backbone of the reef is formed by the so-called 'stony corals' or Madreporaria. Most stony corals have, within the tissues of the polyps, single-celled algae called 'zooxanthellae'. These photosynthesize, like all plants, and provide the coral polyps with oxygen, a by-product of photosynthesis. This greatly benefits the polyps but it means that the stony corals that form the reef are limited to shallow water, where the light is good enough for the zooxanthellae to photosynthesize. By becoming dependent on plants they have accepted one of the limitations of plants – a need for light.

All corals consist of millions of tiny coral animals, each one resembling a miniature sea anemone, or an immobile upside-down jellyfish. These individuals are called polyps, and they each secrete a limestone case. The accumulated limestone cases of innumerable coral polyps, past and present, build up the reef structure. Each coral colony is formed by one original polyp that replicates itself over and over again.

Overleaf left
Offshore from this Fijian island can be seen the shallow markings of a coral reef. The reefs of the South Pacific are particularly rich in shark species and the island natives respect the sharks. In many areas, sharks are thought to be reincarnated ancestors.

Overleaf right
General view of a Pacific reef in Milne Bay, Papua New Guinea. In the foreground are two examples of the soft coral *Sarcophyton trocheliophorum*. The one on the right is feeding in the current with its polyps extended; the one on the left has retracted its polyps. Behind are the finger-like projections of the stony coral known as staghorn coral. There are tell-tale signs that the current is particularly rich in organic nutrients: not only have clouds of damselfish and fairy basslets left the protective safety of the corals to feed, but also burgundy-purple feather-stars, which normally only come out at night, have clambered onto the upper parts of the staghorn coral to claim their share.

There are hundreds of different species of coral. Some, such as the brain coral (it looks like a human brain), are robust and can thrive in turbulent waters. Others, such as the delicately branched elkhorn coral of the Atlantic, are more sensitive and live only in sheltered waters. The common names for some stony corals suggest their various shapes – star coral, flower coral, fungus coral, staghorn coral, mushroom coral, cactus coral, finger coral. The delicate colours of these corals is legendary and the stony corals form the basis of an immensely beautiful and complex environment. Other kinds of coral, worms, snails and other molluscs, shrimps, moss animals (bryozoans), starfish, sea urchins and sea squirts have all adapted to life on the reef, and many have colours as outrageous as their background. In addition there are the dazzling hosts of teleost fish, turtles and, in some parts of the world, sea snakes. And the cartilaginous fish, the sharks and rays, are also here, though not so brightly dressed.

The way in which sharks have adapted to life on the reef makes them of special interest. The coral reef, for all its abundant food sources, is a place of great specialization: sharks of the reef must compete not only with each other, but also with many other kinds of predator. And the intended prey, unless injured or dead, is not easily taken. Wonderful varieties of camouflage, defence, speed and evasion are the norm, and the coral itself offers an abundance of hiding places.

To find a reef on which these hierarchies of life are all present is not as easy as it might seem. Overfishing (with nets, lines, spearguns and even explosives) and general pollution, have

Right
Coral reef animals have developed many means of protection from predators. These reef silversides *Allanetta harringtonensis* are constantly preyed upon by other fish, grouper and jack in particular, but their sheer numbers ensure that the school survives for some time. Though the fish in this school are too small to interest most sharks, the larger fish that feed on them are not.

Below
Sharks compete for food with other predators on the reef. These include many species of grouper, some of which reach impressive size. These grouper from the Great Barrier Reef are known as potato cod *Epinephelus tukula* and are 1.5 metres (nearly 5 feet) in length. They are relatively slow swimmers and to catch small fish they lie in ambush, waiting to suck passers-by into their mouths with a powerful inhalation of water. Or, at night, they hunt in the coral gullies vacuuming up sleeping fish. Their mottled coloration serves as camouflage, and they can rapidly vary the proportions of brown and white. The one in the foreground has turned quite pale, possibly as a warning signal to me.

The epaulette sharks are a small group of bottom-dwelling sharks found in the tropical waters of Australia and New Guinea. 'Epaulette' refers to the dark patches on the sides of the shark, which may appear to be enormous eyes and so deter larger sharks from attempting to eat them. Epaulette sharks are small, less than 1 metre (3 feet) in length, and poor swimmers. The shark *above* is *Hemiscyllium ocellatum* at rest during the day on the Great Barrier Reef. To the *right* is *H. freycineti* from New Guinea. It is foraging at night on the shallow seabed.

destroyed many reefs, and affected most of the others, even in the farthest corners of the world. Many reefs are smashed up with iron bars to provide chunks of coral that can be bought as 'souvenirs', to collect dust in faraway houses. Although there have been efforts to protect various reefs, the destruction has continued. On the reefs of the Sudan, coral-collecting and spear-fishing are banned, but the rules are largely unenforced. In the Florida Keys, a large area of reef has been turned into a protected park – the John Pennekamp Park. You are not allowed to take anything out of the park – unless you happen to be a fisherman, in which case you can catch as much as you want. Needless to say, this reef too has been affected.

The vastness of the Great Barrier Reef, off Australia, has allowed for a different solution. In some reef areas, fishing and spearfishing are allowed. In others, only diving is allowed. A third group of reefs are open only to scientists. Finally, there is a fourth group of reefs that are completely closed off to humans. Such drastic methods are necessary if the full complement of reef life is to be preserved.

To witness a reef in its natural state, one must go far beyond the influences not only of pollution, but also of modern fishing methods. Where there is a modern hotel there is likely to be increased fishing for the hotel menu, and even small-scale fishing can greatly affect the local reefs. Though they may appear healthy, the sharks have gone. Perhaps it is because the available prey has fallen below a critical level, or just because the persistent presence of divers unsettles the sharks. Resort divers have often told me how the local sharks seem to move away after a while and not return.

In order to photograph pristine coral reefs and, as far as possible, the local sharks, I spent three months in the South Pacific at the end of 1984. Not only do the South Pacific reefs include some of the finest in the world, but the sharks are there in abundance. It is difficult to make a dive without seeing at least one shark.

One of the most commonly found sharks on coral reefs throughout the South Pacific, as well as the Indian Ocean and Red Sea, is the whitetip reef shark *Triaenodon obesus*. This is an inoffensive and easily identified shark: the apex of the first dorsal fin and the upper lobe of the tail are both tipped in white. Not only that, the whitetip reef shark (or reef whitetip) has a curious-looking rat-like face, and swims with a pronounced sway of the body. During the day, the whitetip is often to be found lying at rest on the bottom, sometimes out in the open, sometimes hidden under coral. Occasionally you will find several lying together in a crevice, one on top of the other.

The reef whitetip does not attain a great size – 1.5 metres (5 feet) is typical and very few are larger. On the whole they are either shy or entirely disinterested in divers, but they can be aggressive when a speared fish is in the water. On one occasion I was snorkelling along a reef when I had the distinct impression that I was being followed. I looked behind me and saw two reef whitetips a few metres behind. As soon as I saw them, they turned also, as if to pretend that they had not been following me. I resumed my swim and, a few minutes later, turned around to see them still behind me, perhaps only 2 metres (6 or 7 feet) away, but avoiding my gaze like amateur private detectives. This ludicrous situation continued for about ten minutes – the little sharks always behind me, always pretending that they were not following me. Of course, they may just have happened to have been swimming in the same direction as me, but to follow so close behind is unusual. It was the only time I have seen such odd behaviour, though others have told me of the same thing happening to them.

Reef whitetips tend to swim close to the bottom, unlike many other sharks that will soar into the open water. They are doubtless preyed upon by larger sharks, such as the tiger shark. Given their ability to rest under coral heads, darting into crevices is likely to be their defence against predation. Whitetips feed mainly on reef fish, probably snatching fish that are lying in holes at rest. They also take octopuses, crabs and lobsters.

The largest reef whitetip I have ever seen was about 2 metres (6 feet 6 inches) in length – very large for the species. This was on a spectacular reef in the Coral Sea, beyond the Great Barrier Reef, called Osprey Reef. The north wall of the reef comes to an underwater point at about 30 metres (100 feet). Over this point, about a dozen full-sized grey reef sharks *Carcharhinus amblyrhynchos* are usually found patrolling, together with six or seven silvertip sharks *Carcharhinus albimarginatus*. The grey reef sharks are about 2 metres (6 feet 6 inches) long, and the silvertips somewhat larger. Both species are far more powerful and active predators than the reef whitetip. However, on the occasion that I dived there, and we took dead fish down to feed the sharks, this particular whitetip was the first shark in to grab the bait, and the least timid in the presence of divers. In fact, for the first few minutes, it took up position at the bait and was dominant over the larger and more powerful sharks.

Though I have many pictures of reef whitetips, I remember the occasion vividly when I took the picture in this book, because the behaviour of the shark was so unusual. It was on a reef in the North Coral Sea about 200 kilometres (124 miles) from the Australian mainland. The *Reef Explorer*, the boat we were diving from, was anchored in the lagoon of Bougainville Reef. It was just beginning to grow dark and I decided to make one more dive. I kitted up and entered the water, swimming the 100 metres (110 yards) to the drop-off. I had already dived here in the afternoon, and was familiar with the scenery. The coral dropped to great depths ahead of me. I had dived the drop-off to 50 metres (165 feet) that afternoon, and found great sea fans, called gorgonians, webbed across a gulley. Now I was going to stay in the shallows and potter around as the sky gradually grew darker.

The great wheeling schools of jacks were still there, forming complex patterns in one place, before swarming a short distance to reform again. I could also see the reef whitetip shark that I had noticed earlier, but he had paid me no attention in the afternoon and seemed unlikely to do so now. Out in the darkness of the open water, I could make out the shape of a dog-tooth tuna, and the gliding shadows of a couple of grey reef sharks. Their round bellies indicated that they were pregnant, or well-fed, or both. As it grew darker, so other fish formed into schools, as a defence against predation. I began to feel uneasy. The jacks were tightly packed one next to another. The reef sharks were swimming back and forth, still visible,

apparently waiting for it to get a little darker. I suspected that they had their eyes on the jacks, which were now compressed into a tight anxious mass. The whitetip was also beginning to swim faster, back and forth over the coral. He began to take an interest in me, though I was far bigger than him. Nevertheless, he swam past me quite close, before turning and coming in again. It was too dark to focus my camera so I guessed the distance, and fired off a shot. He came in again to investigate and I pressed the shutter button again, but I was not really thinking about photography at that moment. It was unusual for a whitetip to come in so close, or so often, and by now I felt decidedly uneasy. If he was so incautious, might the larger grey reef sharks also switch their attention to me? In haste, I beat a retreat to the boat. I had hoped to see the grey reef sharks attack the jacks, but

The whitetip reef shark is a common shark on the reefs of the Indo-Pacific. Divers soon learn to recognize their local whitetips as these sharks stay in the same area for long periods of time. Usually inoffensive, this individual was photographed at dusk and was very inquisitive.

it was now almost dark and I had no wish to be around if they were dashing after the jacks in the darkness.

That evening, after dinner, I wandered out to the stern of the boat. There were some bright lights on that lit up the water around the boat. I heard a splashing noise from the water and looked over the side to see an impressive spectacle. Flying fish were being attracted to the boat's lights, like moths to the flames of a candle. They would fly out of the water and glide towards the boat, only to crash into the side and float, stunned on the surface. About half-a-dozen grey reef sharks were cruising slowly around, eating the flying fish as they lay dazed on the surface. I very much wanted to get into the water and photograph the sharks feeding, but could not summon the nerve. It takes a special sort of courage to dive among feeding sharks at night.

In the daytime, hunting around in crevices on the reef can occasionally be productive, since many nocturnal sharks rest under coral canopies. One day I was diving a shallow section of reef in northern Fiji at a place where the bottom consisted of sand and isolated coral heads. I saw one particular coral head and – I do not know why – became convinced that there was a shark resting under it. Ignoring this feeling, I resisted the temptation to swim over and have a look. As I investigated other coral heads, I saw that many of them had large, empty gullies running through their bases. Eventually I made my way over to the coral head that I had been perversely ignoring, and, looking underneath, saw a big grey tail resting under it on the sand. The tail was nearly a metre (about 3 feet) long, so I guessed that, whatever it belonged to must be well over 2 metres (6 feet 6 inches) in length. I was pretty sure that it must be a shark known as the tawny shark *Nebrius concolor*, a close relative of the nurse shark. I swam around the other side of the coral formation to see if I could find the head of this resting animal. There was a narrow passage that led in under the coral. The shark was well inside the coral gulley and not yet visible. I did not like the idea of squeezing my way in under the coral and getting trapped with an anxious shark, but the desire to get a photograph overcame common sense, and so, very gingerly, I started working my way inside the coral, my tank scraping the roof above me. I worked my way in about 2 metres (2 yards) to where the tunnel turned at a right angle. I slowly looked around the corner, holding my breath so as not to disturb the shark with my bubbles. I was greeted by a big, grey head with tiny, beady eyes staring at me. It was, indeed, a large tawny shark. Then it turned around in its cavern, placing the long curved tail in my face. Now I was worried that it would swim out of the opposite exit, so I wriggled backwards out through the passage I had entered, and swam around to the other side. By the time I got there, the shark had turned around again – all I could see was the long, grey tail resting on the sand. Muttering a curse, I swam back to the long passageway and re-entered – to be greeted by the tail again. And so we continued, the shark greeting my every approach with its tail. I knew that, sooner or later, it would have had enough of my disturbing it and would swim away. But I hoped that I would be in front of the right exit and would manage to get a picture. I wasn't. And I didn't.

Hammerhead sharks are frequent visitors to the Pacific reefs. Whenever I see a hammerhead underwater I think it looks as if it has come from another planet. And yet I am struck by how something so

Divers are often warned not to touch anything that moves so slowly that they could touch it. This is sound advice. If the creature does not rely on speed to escape a predator, then it has other defences. Venomous spines are popular among certain reef fish, and this widespread lionfish species *Pterois volitans* is a good example. Lionfish feed by suddenly darting forward to engulf small prey. Their long, elegant fins break up their fish-like appearance. Indeed, they tend to be found where corals are particularly rich and varied, and in such places they blend well into the background.

The indentations on the front edge of the head of the scalloped hammerhead are characteristic. The strange head shape of hammerheads may act as a forward planing surface that increases the sharks' manoeuvrability, or with eyes located on the outer edges of the hammer, the sharks may have an improved capacity to judge distance. With the sensory organs in the snout dispersed along the whole of the hammer, and the nostrils located close to the eyes, a hammerhead is continually sampling a larger area of water than a shark with the more normal head shape.

ugly can be so beautiful. The most commonly seen species on Indo-Pacific reefs is the scalloped hammerhead, *Sphyrna lewini*. Indeed, this is probably the most abundant hammerhead species, being common in tropical waters throughout the world. However, the most magnificent hammerhead is the great hammerhead, *Sphyrna mokarran*.

Although I have seen several great hammerheads underwater, one occasion in particular stands out. It was in the Coral Sea again, on one of the isolated reefs that jut out of the ocean. The bottom sloped at about 45° downwards and consisted of squat grey coral formations. I was planning to dive deep, because occasionally I would see something incredible far down that outweighed the many uneventful deep dives. My first impression however, was that this would be a dull dive. Nevertheless, I set my watch and headed off down the slope. The same uninteresting coral formations persisted. At 50 metres (165 feet) I stopped and looked around. There was nothing there but the coral. The water was clear, and I could see for some distance in all directions. I took my diving knife out of its sheath and clanged it against my tank a few times, in the hope of attracting a shark. Almost immediately, a reef whitetip and a couple of grey reef sharks appeared from nowhere. I paid them little attention as they kept their distance, and after a while I decided to return to the shallows. I was just about to set off when I noticed a grey movement at the limit of visibility, far down the slope. Something down there was swimming towards me. There was an ungainliness about its movement – it was jerky, lacking in grace. I immediately realized that this must be a hammerhead, and a big one. Hammerheads swim with this apparently clumsy motion, throwing the head from side to side – since the eyes are located on the side of the head, this is how they see forward. You can identify a hammerhead just by the movement of the body, long before you can see the shape of the head. Even at a distance I could tell that this particular animal was large, bigger than any I had seen before. I lifted up my camera and waited for it to come in. It was swimming slowly – no hint of aggression – and I felt instinctively that it would swim by for one look and then

Left
The angelfish include some of the most elaborately coloured fish on the reef. This is the Indo-Pacific emperor angelfish *Pomacanthus imperator*, photographed on a reef off New Guinea. The coloration breaks up the shape of the fish, and the eye is hidden in the thick dark line that runs across the head. There is also a strong defensive spine (blue in colour), just before the pectoral fin.

Above
The grey angelfish *Pomacanthus arcuatus* of western Atlantic reefs is a drab grey in contrast. Its flattened body allows it to slip into gaps in coral at the approach of danger and its shape has some similarity to the sea fans on the reefs where it is found. These are visible behind the angelfish. Grey angelfish often swim in pairs on the reef and will venture out onto exposed areas of sand – something the other, more colourful angelfish will not do.

leave. It was still a long way off, but growing larger and larger. I could see the white front edge of the hammer-like head, jerking from side to side, and the grey-silver arch of the back up to the tall dorsal fin. It was so much larger than any other shark I had seen before that I could not judge how far away it was. Nor did I have anything to measure it against. There was just the featureless grey coral. It looked as if it was almost on top of me, it was so big, but in fact it was still some distance off.

To get a picture I knew I must wait until it was in range of my strobe. Experience told me that, at any moment, the shark would turn off at an angle and swim away – but on this occasion experience was wrong. The hammerhead just carried on towards me. I looked through my camera and, when the animal seemed to fill the whole field of view, I took a picture. Lowering my camera, I could see the shark was still some distance off, slowly pumping its way towards me, the head tossing from side to side. I realized that it was on a collision course with me, though for some reason I did not feel threatened. I swam sideways and the shark must have fractionally altered its course, because suddenly it was beside me. The broad flank of the massive animal seemed close enough to touch. Now I had some sense of the hammerhead's size – and I felt dwarfed by it. The body seemed at least twice my length and then there was the long, swaying arc of the tail. It seemed to take an eternity to pass me, but at last it was gone, on its way up the reef, eventually fading into the distance.

How big was it? I cannot say exactly, but the size alone told me it was a great hammerhead, and the pictures later confirmed it. This specimen was at least 4 metres (13 feet), maybe nearer 5 metres (17

SHARKS OF THE SHALLOWS 87

feet). And great hammerheads are known to get larger still.

When the film was processed a couple of months later – heartbreak. The first shot, of the animal approaching, was a failure: the film had not advanced properly and the shark was cut in two. However, the second shot was sharp, showing that the animal was farther away than I had thought and, therefore, every bit as large. The deep mating scars on the flank showed that it was a female, recently mated.

I have come across other divers who have been approached very closely by large hammerheads. On a few occasions the sharks have actually bumped into the divers before swimming off. Certainly, when sharks grow this large, they tend not to be as timid as their smaller brethren. In some parts of the world, hammerheads are considered to be the most dangerous of the local sharks, though I

A great hammerhead, the biggest I have ever seen, dwarfs me as she passes, her black eye regarding me with diminishing interest as she slowly pumps away, head tossing from side to side. The deep scars in her flank identify her as a mature female and I can only guess at her size.

have never been harassed by one. However, Stan Spielman, an ophthalmologist in Miami who has worked on the vision of sharks, told me of an alarming experience he had with a great hammerhead. He was snorkelling in shallow water in Elliot Key in Florida, when an agitated and aggressive great hammerhead approached him. It swung its head from side to side as it approached, and what struck Stan was how confusing this was to him: with a normal shark swimming straight at you, you know which way to turn. But with this swinging head movement, Stan could not tell at what angle the shark might come at him. He suggested that this head movement might be equally confusing to a school of fish. The hammerhead might, by tossing its head from side to side, break up a school so that they become confused and scatter in all directions – making them that much easier to catch.

If you are diving on a coral reef in the Indo-Pacific or Red Sea, and you see a medium-sized grey shark, with a dark edge to its tail, then the chances are that it is the grey reef shark, *Carcharhinus amblyrhynchos*. Actually, there is some dispute as to whether the grey reef shark of the Red Sea and western Indian Ocean is a variant on the Pacific version, or is in fact a distinct species, but I will come to that in the next chapter. The Pacific grey reef shark has some fascinating features to its biology.

These sharks do not grow very large. Although they may reach more than 2 metres (6 feet 6 inches) in length, most are less than this, 1.5 metres (5 feet) being typical. Of all the grey reef sharks that I have seen, only a few were any larger.

Grey reef sharks are not found solely on reefs, but this is where

The zebra shark *Stegostoma varium* is found on reefs from the Red Sea to Australia. Juveniles are striped but in adults the stripes diminish to spots. This individual is about 2 metres (6 feet 6 inches) in length, and was photographed in the Coral Sea, resting on the bottom, a typical day-time posture. At night, zebra sharks are more active and feed on small fish, crustaceans and molluscs.

The Threat Display of the Grey Reef Shark

The normal swimming posture of the grey reef shark is shown, *top*. In a mild display, *centre*, the pectoral fins are lowered and the shark swims slowly with a stiffened body motion. Sometimes the shark will swim in tight circles or figures of eight. The threat display at its most acute is shown, *bottom*. The pectorals are lowered and the back hunched; the snout is lifted and the mouth held open. Frozen in this extraordinary posture, the shark will begin to sink towards the bottom. A moment later it will dash forward to attack its protagonist with a slashing bite.

It is not known if all grey reef sharks perform this display. It is documented from island groups in the mid-Pacific, but the full display has not been recorded in Indian Ocean and Red Sea sharks.

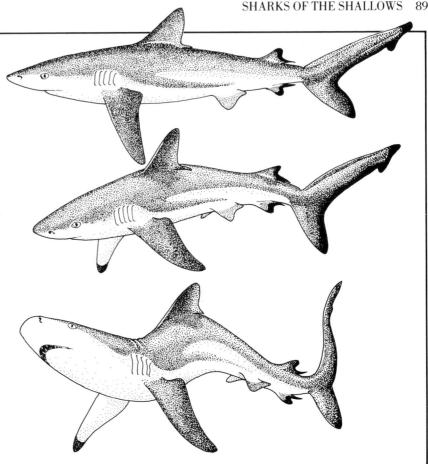

divers most often encounter them. Sometimes those encounters end in disaster. In 1961, two divers, Ron Church and Jim Stewart, were exploring a coral reef off Wake Island in the mid-Pacific. A grey reef shark approached. It became agitated, swimming with a clumsy motion, the head swaying back and forth almost as much as the tail. Then it sped past Stewart only to swerve back and bite him, inflicting a serious injury on his arm. Other divers have been bitten under similar circumstances, after the shark has gone into this swimming pattern. The sharks do not usually produce this behaviour unless they are followed or harassed by a diver. Once, on a dive off an isolated pinnacle in the Great Barrier Reef, I came across a group of about eight grey reef sharks that were holding a position at the end of the reef. There was a strong current and I had to pull myself over the coral to make progress against it. I half-swam and half-dragged myself towards the sharks, and they retreated a little way, keeping in a tight group. When I continued to follow them, one of the sharks separated from the others and took up a position about halfway between me and the group. It dropped its pectoral fins so that they pointed almost straight downwards and started swimming, with a stiff body motion, back and forth in a figure-of-eight pattern. At this, I immediately beat a retreat – or rather let the current carry me away along the reef. I knew that to try to photograph the shark would be very risky – there is a case of a diver being attacked by a shark when he photographed this display. The firing of the strobe could well have triggered the attack.

Don Nelson has made a fascinating study of this behaviour by grey reef sharks in the Pacific. He built a small, one-man wet submarine (the person inside uses scuba gear) which he christened the S.O.S., or Shark Observation Submersible. At Enewetak, in the Marshall Islands, he pursued grey reef sharks and other species from within the relative safety of the submersible. He found that the grey reef sharks were most likely to display if he performed what he called an orientated pursuit – the submersible following the shark's every movement. Three other species of shark were pursued in a similar manner – the silvertip *Carcharhinus albimarginatus*, the blackfin *Carcharhinus melanopterus* and the reef whitetip shark *Triaenodon obesus*. Of these three species, one silvertip performed what he termed a mild threat display, while the other sharks kept their distance or swam rapidly away. However, with the grey reef sharks, over half of those followed went into the stiff swimming pattern. Those that displayed most strongly would often dash in and bite the submersible. Don has shown me film shot during the experiments. A displaying grey reef shark would start swimming very stiffly, the pectorals down, the back hunched. Often the snout would be lifted upwards. It might swim back and forth very slowly in front of the submersible. In the most extreme cases, the shark would stop swimming and freeze in the water before it began to sink, like a giant leaf, towards the bottom. Then it would burst into action, dashing in to bite the submersible one or more times.

Don believes that this threat display, which warns that an attack may follow, has been developed as a defence against predation by larger sharks. Grey reef sharks are often found in exposed reef areas where larger species of shark can occur, and these might be tempted

Above
A 2 metre (6 feet 6 inches) silvertip flashes past me on the reef. Silvertips are the most beautifully coloured requiem sharks with silvery white edges to their fins. This one has had a chunk of his first dorsal fin removed by another shark, perhaps an aggressive grey reef shark.

Right
Grey reef sharks on a Pacific reef attack dead fish that have been brought down to feed them. The resulting 'feeding frenzy' is artificial as many sharks compete for a limited amount of food. Under these circumstances I have never seen the sharks bite each other.

to include the grey reef shark in their diet.

But why do the other sharks which Don studied not show the same display? Blackfin and whitetip are both small, but the blackfin likes very shallow water, and may well dart into the shallows to avoid a larger shark. The whitetip can hide in a hole in the coral. Silvertips, on the other hand, grow much larger than grey reef sharks, and may be less prone to predation by other sharks. Thus it is only the grey reef shark that needs to see off larger, predatory sharks in this way.

Grey reef sharks tend to congregate in certain areas on a reef, and taking dead fish down to feed such gatherings invariably produces dramatic results. The sharks rush in, competing with each other to get the food. The so-called 'shark frenzy' is, in fact, an artificially produced rivalry among the sharks for the dead fish. On one occasion, when I was photographing these sharks feeding, I had my strobe bitten as it was recharging – a repeat of the Bahamas experience. When a couple of sharks then butted me from behind, I felt that the time had come to retreat.

Of the 350 living species of shark, all but three actively hunt large prey. The three exceptions are the filter-feeders – the basking shark *Cetorhinus maximus*, the whale shark *Rhincodon typus* and the little known megamouth shark *Megachasma pelagios*. The whale shark is distributed worldwide in tropical seas. It is the world's biggest fish, though no one really knows how large whale sharks can get. Certainly they reach 13 or 14 metres (about 45 feet) and may even attain 18 metres (60 feet) in length. Sightings of whale sharks by divers are very rare and have passed into the mythology of the sport as the ultimate experience. Despite its huge size, the whale shark was not known to science until 1828, and not photographed underwater until 1950, when a startled Hans Hass came across an 8-metre (26-foot) specimen in the Red Sea. I never dreamed that I would see one. In December of 1984, on the last leg of my tropical diving trip in the South Pacific, I went to Milne Bay, on the extreme eastern tip of Papua New Guinea. Here I spent two weeks diving with Bob Halstead, an Englishman who operates a diving club in Port Moresby and takes divers on expeditions to the virgin reefs of Papua.

Each morning, as we prepared to leave another village and board the boat for the day's diving, Bob would unroll a chart of dubious accuracy to discuss where we would dive. The chart was festooned with reefs, some of which he had already sampled, but most of which were unvisited. We were halfway into our trip and I was already convinced that I was diving the finest reefs that I had ever seen. What other reefs boast as exceptional, these reefs have as standard. And what these reefs have as exceptional is unbelievable.

One morning Bob was gazing at his chart and trying to decide which reef to pick. I jokingly asked him if he knew a reef where we might find manta rays, hammerheads and silvertip sharks, and if he could throw in a whale shark, I would be most grateful. With barely a smile, he said he knew just the place, though it would take us a couple of hours to get there.

Later in the morning we dropped anchor a few hundred metres off a rainforest shore. Below the boat, the water changed suddenly from green to blue-black, declaring the boundary between reef and deep water. About 50 metres (55 yards) along the reef there was a kink in the coral where it jutted out into a point. Bob advised me to swim to

The whale shark, vast and inquisitive, returns for a second look at me before vanishing along the reef with startling speed. Although basically filter feeders, whale sharks have been observed to feed on small tuna by rising vertically up through the water and engulfing the tuna which were themselves feeding on smaller fish. Whale sharks are thought to be migratory, their movements determined by the plankton blooms that occur due to seasonal changes.

the corner, position myself in the coral and wait. He assured me that, sooner or later, something would turn up.

I followed his instructions and positioned myself at the corner in 10 metres (33 feet) of water. I laid my cameras out around me. Below, the reef stretched away, a contorted and tangled mass of coral, disappearing down into the gullet of the ocean. The rich and complex corals beckoned me to follow them down, but I resisted. I ignored the gaudy angelfish and butterfly fish that hovered around me. Instead, I prepared to wait, even though I felt impatient. It was absurd to expect a whale shark, but still. . .

After a few minutes I decided to do my knife-clanging trick. It might bring in a hammerhead. As I banged my knife against my tank, the crude sound battered its way across the silent coral and out into the open water. Even as I was putting my knife back into its sheath, I saw something. It was black, about 1.5 metres (5 feet) long: a horizontal black line above the coral, swaying from side to side, approaching me. With a shock I realized that it was the mouth of a whale shark coming straight towards me. Behind it, the outline of the body was becoming apparent.

I grabbed the camera with the widest lens and waited. The enormous shark approached powerfully, at speed. I could only guess at its size from the age it took to pass overhead, like a spaceship. I took a picture, but still it continued to pass over me. The head, then the broad, pale belly, and eventually, the long, swaying tail. The grace and strength were breathtaking. The swept-back tail, like the sail of an Egyptian dhow, flowed with power. I had heard reports that whale sharks are sluggish, but this one was moving with the effortless speed of a giant reef shark. Two lazy beats of the tail and it was gone, travelling on along the reef. The speed seemed impossible for the bulk. I was trembling with excitement, wondering if it had ever really been there. The reef was unchanged, the little fish oblivious in the silence. The only evidence was in my camera.

It occurred to me that the whale shark had gone off in the direction of another group of divers. They might alarm it, and it might return. I turned and suddenly there it was, coming straight back towards me. In a few seconds it had turned completely around. I wondered if the others had seen it. As it came on with the same remarkable speed, I turned my camera to the vertical, just to get the whole thing in. It had to be 9 or 10 metres (30 or 33 feet) long. I straightened up to get even closer. There was every temptation to shoot, but I waited. It continued to grow in the viewfinder. Wait, wait, wait. When it filled the viewfinder and seemed to block out the daylight, I released the shutter. With the momentum of a bus it powered past me and was gone.

A few minutes later Bob appeared. He gestured by placing his hand on his forehead. I realized that he was signalling that he had seen a swordfish or a marlin. I responded with the only signal I could think of for a whale shark – stretching my arms out as far as I could.

CHAPTER FOUR

—*THE*—
SHARKS
—*OF*—
SANGANEB

The coral reefs of the Red Sea are famed for their luxuriance, with a richness of marine life that is in stark contrast to the coastal deserts around them. They also have a healthy supply of sharks.

Of all the Red Sea reefs, the coral atoll of Sanganeb, located 31 km (19 miles) northeast of Port Sudan and 15 km (9 miles) out from the arid African coast, is one of the richest and most exciting for a diver, its isolation ensuring that its wildlife is well preserved. The local lighthouse keepers catch an occasional fish, but, apart from them and the resident pair of ospreys, the reef is left relatively untouched. Like other atoll reefs, Sanganeb is basically circular in shape, enclosing a central lagoon: such atolls are formed by corals establishing themselves on the crests of submerged volcanoes.

Jack Jackson has been leading diving expeditions to Sanganeb atoll for over ten years. He originally investigated the reef by working in conjunction with a local fisherman who occasionally ventured out from Port Sudan. The fisherman would show Jack where the fishing was best and Jack would dive the spot – invariably the best dive sites overlapped with the best fishing grounds. Jack has, over the years, built up an intimate knowledge of the reef – not only in terms of its physical features, but also in terms of what animal is likely to be found where. This was to prove invaluable to me when I turned up and wanted to find sharks.

My first trip to Sanganeb was in the summer of 1984, when the local heat was at its most fierce. In fact, the midday temperature was so hot that the only thing to do was to spend the time in the water, if not diving, then snorkelling. Gradually, with Jack's help, I built up a picture of the reef's outline. It comes to two points underwater, one at the north, the other at the south-west corner of the atoll – underwater coral promontories that jut out from the main reef. The north point goes out in a series of stages. It starts at about 25 metres (82 feet) deep, and is 80 metres (88 yards) wide at this point. As the promontory continues, so it drops deeper and narrows. One hundred metres from the surface coral, it is about 50 metres (165 feet) deep. It carries on down, getting deeper and deeper, beyond the limits of the scuba diver.

Over this point can be found rich schools of fish including jacks

The lighthouse of Sanganeb warns passing ships of the reefs that encircle it. The reefs are majestic and teeming with fish.

Below The Sanganeb coral atoll is oval in shape. The lighthouse with two long jetties (1) stands in the southern half of the lagoon. Whitetip reef sharks can be found almost anywhere on the outer reef wall, but it is at the underwater promontories of the north (2) and south-west points (3) that other sharks gather. Both extend from the backbone of the reef out into open water, and are remarkably rich in animal life.

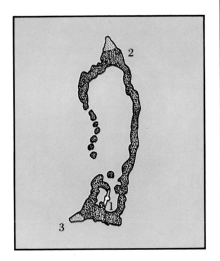

and barracuda. Also, the local variety of grey reef shark is nearly always seen, patrolling along the point. An occasional scalloped hammerhead *Sphyrna lewini* is encountered, but far more spectacular are the large schools of scalloped hammerheads. Jack told me that in the previous summer he had made many dives on the north point and seen the hammerheads in schools of thirty or more on almost every dive. The trouble was that when he was at 50 metres (165 feet) the hammerheads tended to be far above him, and when he was in the shallows, he would spot them far below.

The south-west point juts out into deep water for about 100 metres (110 yards) but does not drop as deep as the north point. It begins at about 25 metres (82 feet) and, at the end, is just over 30 metres (100 feet) deep. This stretch is populated by a staggering variety of fish. Dozens of large brownmarbled grouper have taken up residence in the coral caverns. Schools of barracuda, jacks and rainbow runners mass and swarm overhead. Grey reef sharks patrol the point and an occasional scalloped hammerhead passes by. Jack told me that there was always so much going on at the top of the point that he had never bothered to look deeper.

The grey reef shark of the western Indian Ocean and the Red Sea differs from the Pacific variety in several ways. The former has a conspicuous white marking on the back edge of the first dorsal fin. This is considerably reduced, or absent altogether in the Pacific shark. It also tends to have a blunter snout than the Pacific version, and one less tooth on each side of the upper jaw. Finally, it is thought to be considerably less aggressive than the Pacific grey reef shark. For these reasons, it was once believed to be a distinct species, *Carcharhinus wheeleri*. Now however, most experts feel that the similarities outweigh the differences and that the two are in fact one species – *Carcharhinus amblyrhynchos*.

Jack told me that sharks could be encountered at any place on the

THE SANGANEB REEF
This is a diagrammatic representation of the activity on the south-west point. Along the promontory are patches of sand and clusters of coral formations. Soft corals (1) billow in the strong current that sweeps along the reef. Large grouper (2) hover in the coral gullies while schools of jacks (3), barracuda (4) and rainbow runners cloud the water above the coral. Grey reef sharks (5) usually patrol along the promontory while below them, in the cool depths beneath the thermocline, silvertips (6), tiger sharks (7) and hammerheads (8) roam and gather.

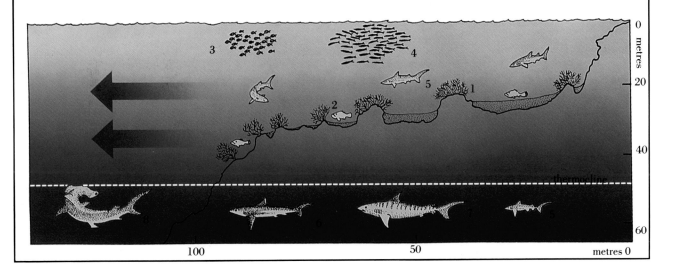

reef, but that they tended to congregate over these two promontories. Both points can have strong currents flowing across them, making diving difficult. However, the strong currents also mean that there is a great concentration of food at these places. The current sweeps along the reef wall – from the north along the western edge of the reef, and from the east on the southern edge. At each of the two points the current is carried along the promonontory – where all the predators and schooling fish mass – and then continues out to sea. All the nutrients picked up along the reef will pass off the reef at these points. Hence the gatherings of smaller fish and sharks.

I was anxious to dive on the north point and search out the schooling hammerheads. But anchoring there is very difficult, as the prevailing wind comes from the north, and tends to push an anchored boat onto the coral. Jack felt that we would be lucky to dive there more than once or twice in the season, and he was right. On the few occasions that the weather was flat calm, we made it to the north point, but although I spotted a few large hammerheads far down on the point, I did not get anywhere near them.

On the other hand, the south-west point is nearly always diveable – you can anchor on the western side of the reef, or move a little around the corner and anchor on the southern edge of the reef. It is even possible to get into the water at the south jetty and swim along the southern edge of the reef to the south-west point. So most of my shark photography at Sanganeb was centred on the south-west point.

The thermocline at Sanganeb can usually be found at a depth of about 50 metres (165 feet). Below this, in the chill depths, other sharks can be seen. Jack told me that he had seen a few tiger sharks, over the years, at a depth of 70 metres (230 feet) off the south wall of the reef. I made several such deep dives in the hope of seeing them and, on a few occasions, saw the silhouettes of large, fat-bellied sharks moving through the gloom. They were requiem sharks, but too large to be reef sharks. It was hard to identify them, but they were definitely not tiger sharks. Diving to such depths is of questionable wisdom, and it is too dark to get a worthwhile photograph, so I soon abandoned these very deep dives.

I continued to go down to 50 or 60 metres (between 160 and 200 feet) however, and on a couple of dawn dives below the thermocline at the south-west point, I was rewarded by an extraordinary sight. The water above the thermocline was almost dark as the sun was just beginning to rise. As soon as I dropped down into the colder water, I could see the ghostly shapes of small hammerheads moving in a layer just below the thermocline. They were not exactly schooling, being fairly widely dispersed. But they were everywhere I looked, coming towards me and then fading away again. It was as if the upper limit of the colder water was the surface of their world and that to swim through the thermocline would have been as unlikely as if they had crawled out onto the land. Although they were plentiful, these small hammerheads were also shy, and they kept their distance. I soon realized that I was not going to get a decent photograph of them.

The grey reef sharks were equally elusive. Diving on the south-west point I would see them moving through the stiff current with considerably less difficulty than I was experiencing. Clinging to the coral to maintain my position, I would wonder how to get close enough to these sharks to photograph them. They were completely

On the south-west point of Sanganeb the reef wall is studded with colourful outcrops of coral and sponge. Here a parrotfish passes over what was once a formation of stony corals but is now covered in other sedentary creatures. A variety of sponges have established themselves in the centre of the formation, while pale orange, soft corals billow in the current. These lack the algae found in most stony corals and survive by filtering out organic material from the passing current. When the current is flowing the soft corals are extended; when the water is slack they withdraw into small, bulbous masses.

Overleaf
Moray eels *Gymnothorax spp.* lurk in the recesses of the coral reef. Powerful and stealthy hunters, they slide through coral gaps in search of prey. Once, Jack Jackson and I were decompressing in the shallows after feeding the reef sharks. The wire frame to which we attach fish was dangling below me. I felt a strong pull on the wire frame and, looking down, saw these two moray eels helping themselves to a few left-over scraps. We estimated the eel on the left to be over 1.5 metres (nearly 5 feet) long.

disinterested in me, and did not deviate from their trance-like patrols. It was a frustrating situation – the sharks were there but I could not move closer to them, nor induce them to come to me. There was only one occasion during that summer of 1984 on which a grey reef shark showed any interest in me, and then it was the kind of interest that I could well have done without. Indeed, this was as frightening an encounter as any I have had with a shark. . . .

I was snorkelling along the coral wall at dusk. The midday wind had died, leaving the surface flat and grey. On the horizon, the setting sun was burning an orange road across the sea towards me. With the sun so low, most of the light bounced off the surface, and it was twilight underwater. The splendid daytime colours of the reef had softened, and the shallow corals were taking on subtle shades of

A coral trout *Cephalopholis miniatus* yawns in a cavern on the reef. The current is flowing through here, revealed by the extended soft coral opposite the coral trout. He has positioned himself near a school of bait fish and, when he gets hungry, will rush through them to feed.

Several Napoleon fish *Cheilinus undulatus* cruise up and down the reef at Sanganeb. This 1.25-metre (4-foot) individual is the largest and has taken up permanent residence on the south-west point. He was the first fish to take offered food and would sometimes grab it before the sharks. He became a regular companion on dives.

mauve and violet. Parrotfish, in their crazy green and purple patterns, swooped in and out of the coral formations, pausing occasionally to crunch their horny beaks on the coral, their staple food. The water was filled with strange sounds as the nightlife of the reef began to stir. There were small, sharp cracking noises and strange, single raps – hidden crustaceans flexing and snapping their joints. Everything seemed to be feeding.

Beyond the vertical coral wall, fish had begun to school. Behind me in the lagoon, I heard the clatter of the lighthouse generator as it started up. I looked up out of the water to see a brief plume of black smoke, and then the four beams of light beginning to circle far above. I ducked back below the surface, returning to the far more extraordinary underwater world. The water was warm, in places even hot, as it streamed off from the shallow lagoon which the sun had baked throughout the day. For the thousandth time I was amazed by the beauty of the reef – that anywhere could be so beautiful.

I rested in a coral niche out of the current and watched the fish. After a few minutes the shy butterflyfish had grown accustomed to me and came a little closer. I wondered if the sharks – somewhere out there – had begun to feed. Minutes passed. As I relaxed, the parrotfish lingered close by.

Then it happened. Five metres below me a grey reef shark streaked by. I had never seen one move so fast, nor appear so agitated. Instinctively I knew that this shark meant trouble. And yet there was something haphazard about the shark's careering, as if it was undirected, in a blind fury. Then it was gone. I remained completely still, hardly breathing, confident that it never knew I was there. I decided to stay a few more minutes, hidden in the coral, before setting off on the long swim back to the jetty. I reckoned that the shark was a hundred metres or so away by now.

Just as I was preparing to leave, I saw the shark again. It was coming up from below this time, charging me, pointed and streamlined. Experience told me that it would veer off before it got too close and then, surely, vanish for good. But it was coming so fast, closing the gap in split-seconds. I pushed my camera towards it, in a slow, feeble gesture of defence. Less than a metre off it swerved to the side, hunching and snapping its jaws, then flicked away, grey and angular, frantically disturbed. The message seemed clear – 'Get out of my territory, I'm feeding!'

Recovering my senses, I started the long, slow swim back to the jetty, gazing into the gloom around me. I hoped that the shark had gone, but I doubted it. It was hunting, and hunting right there. I began to ask myself what I thought I was doing out there, in the middle of nowhere, alone on a reef at dusk. The reef fish swam by, unconcerned.

It seemed as if I had now put a safe distance between me and the shark. It was only just visible, and yet I could still see it darting around in wild arcs, bucking up to the surface, then plunging

From dead ahead the elegant curves of a grey reef shark become hostile. The drab automaton that idly followed the contours of the reef has focussed its attention and now resembles a metallic dart.

downwards, as if chasing some imaginary foe. Its whole body snapped like a whip with the beats of its broad, black-edged tail. As I continued swimmimg, however, I realized that the shark had not left me at all, but was engaged in a frenzied escort. I was at the centre of its tense circling.

Thankfully the shark never came quite so close again, and at last it lost interest in me, as if I had suddenly crossed an invisible boundary. Its frantic movements slackened to a gentle drift behind me. The shark relaxed, its supremacy restored. . . .

When I subsequently related this experience to Don Nelson, he challenged my interpretation – that I was in a territory that the shark was defending. His own work on Pacific grey reef sharks strongly suggests that their hunch display is a response to potential predators. Furthermore, Don has fitted transmitters to grey reef sharks and shown that some move considerable distances. One shark that he tagged on the open water side of the reef at Enewetak, moved 16 km (10 miles) during the first night of its being recorded. It is difficult to reconcile this with the idea that such a shark has a territory to defend. Whatever the reason for this particular shark taking such a dislike to me, the experience was a memorable one. It did nothing to convince me that the Red Sea reef sharks are an amiable lot, and thereafter I took few chances. When the trip came to an end, I had only got a couple of shots of the sharks, cruising in the distance.

The next summer I returned to Sanganeb with Jack and was prepared to tackle the problem of photographing reef sharks afresh. I decided to feed the grey reef sharks on the south-west point, to try to get them to come closer. On the first occasion that I took fish down to them, the large, local napoleon fish – a giant species of wrasse – moved in and grabbed the dead fish while the sharks were dancing around in the background, excited but timid. The next day I went down with Jack to try again. I hovered over the drop-off and cut up a barracuda. I wanted the smell of the fish to drift along the reef and hoped that it might even attract a hammerhead. I glanced up from the bloody cloud I was making to see a tiger shark swimming straight towards me. I dropped the fish and retreated to the reef, and luckily, the tiger shark swam off after that first alarming approach. Jack told me later that it was somewhat larger than me – about 2.5 metres (8 feet) long.

As the days went by and we continued to feed the grey reef sharks, once and sometimes twice a day, it became evident that they were considerably less bold than their Pacific cousins. It would often take many minutes before they came in and grabbed the bait. However, I did make one interesting discovery – that the fish need not be fresh or oozing blood. On one occasion the lighthouse keepers gave us some fried fish to eat. Because we were low on fresh fish with which to feed the sharks, I took our leftovers down. They worked just as well!

When we were not feeding the sharks, I would swim to the end of the point to see if I could find any hammerheads. It was not unusual to see one or two, about 2.5 to 3 metres (8 to 10 feet) in length, vanishing off the point into the deeper water at my approach. Their characteristically jerky, side-to-side swimming motion identified them, even when they were a long way off. Also, there is something about the way in which the sun can, even in deep water, hit the side of a hammerhead's body. It glows briefly in the gloom, a ghostly

Right
On tropical reefs gaudy coloration is the norm. The large fish is a parrotfish *Cetoscarus bicolor* from the Red Sea. Parrotfish derive their name from their beak-like mouths, although their flamboyant colours rival those of parrots. This fish is a mature male; the females of the species are brown with a yellow stripe. Parrotfish graze on algae they find on the coral and often cause damage as they gouge their beaks across it.

Below
A grey reef shark patrols the drop-off at Sanganeb. Grey reef sharks have the compactness, the manoeuvrability and the speed to be the dominant shark predators on the coral reefs of the Indo-Pacific and Red Sea.

silver-white. This happens when the shark tilts its body slightly, so that its flank is square to the sun. It has even been suggested that they tilt their bodies in this way to signal to each other.

After a few dives to the end of the point, during which I usually saw the hammerheads vanishing below me, it became obvious that I ought to look deeper. However, this made for a long, deep dive, and often a tiring one, as there could be a vicious current pulling away from the point. It was easy getting to the end, but a struggle getting back. However, on the third occasion that I dived off the point, I went through the thermocline at 50 metres (165 feet) and saw eight large hammerheads holding a tight formation out in the open water. They were all mature females, and, as they briefly approached me for a look, I could see that they were heavily scarred with bite marks on their bellies and sides – possibly the signs of mating, left by the teeth of the male shark. I managed to photograph them, but was not really satisfied: they were only a small group and I wanted a whole school.

In October of the same year, Jack and I returned for a five-week stay on Sanganeb. This time I brought out with me a home-made shark cage and hired a local fisherman, who would catch fish on which to feed the sharks. I was hoping to attract tiger sharks, hammerheads and even some open-water species such as the oceanic whitetip, *Carcharhinus longimanus*. The idea was to make a soup of the mashed up fish and continually ladle it over the side of the boat to set up a slick – a technique known as 'chumming'. The current should take the slick a considerable distance and attract sharks from far and wide. However, after a few days of trying, nothing turned up. (Sonny Gruber has since told me that chumming does not seem to work very well with sharks in the tropics.) So Jack and I concentrated on the grey reef sharks. There were four in regular attendance: three females, of which two were obviously pregnant, and a slim male. One of the females had three large sharksuckers attached to her that were almost as long as her. These teleost fish are not parasitic, but they attach themselves to larger fish, whales or turtles, by a sucker on their heads, thus saving themselves the trouble of swimming. By hitching a lift on a larger animal, they are carried around to good feeding grounds, and can also prey on the many parasites found on the host's body.

We began to notice certain behavioural features amongst these grey reef sharks. The same female (recognized by a bite in her first dorsal fin) tended to be the most bold, and would come in first to feed. The male would often arrive after the females, and perform some sort of display. He would circle overhead with his pectorals held down while the females gradually moved in on the bait, totally ignoring him. After a few vain attempts to establish his supremacy, he would give up and join them.

One evening a visiting fisherman caught a small grey reef shark and gave it to me, as it was considered inedible. Out of curiosity, I took it down with me the next morning to see if our sharks would eat it. They were waiting expectantly when we got in the water, but as soon as they smelt the dead shark, they fled. In fact, we did not see a shark on the south-west point for three days – an unheard-of situation. On the third day three different grey reef sharks had arrived. They were larger females with fresh mating scars. We only saw two of the old group again, and that was five days after they had

The current is flowing along the south-west point, and the soft corals have extended to filter microscopic particles of food from it. I have placed some dead fish in the coral head. Within moments the grey reef sharks arrive. Smelling the fish they line up in the current before closing in to grab the food.

all vanished. The slim male never returned to the south-west point, though I subsequently saw him (or what I think was him) about a kilometre away, on the south face of the reef.

The trip to Sanganeb ended with my having numerous photographs of the grey reef sharks, but I was still dissatisfied with my scalloped hammerhead shots. The last expedition to Sanganeb was in June 1986 and when I arrived I had still not decided how to proportion my dives. My main aim was to photograph a school of hammerheads, but to dive off the south-west point every day was to use up most of my dives on what might be a futile endeavour. There were plenty of other photographic subjects along the shallow areas of the reef, whereas I could spend the whole month diving deep and end up without a picture. And yet there were so many reasons to think that if there *were* schooling hammerheads off Sanganeb, they were likely to be in deep water off the south-west point. There were more reef sharks there than at the north point, larger schools of barracuda, jacks and other fish, and countless large groupers that scurried off ahead when I dived. All in all, the predators and prey were massed on the south-west point: if it was food the hammerheads were after, that was where they should be.

My first dive off the south-west point that June was an eventful one. As I dropped down through the thermocline, I saw a silvertip, *Carcharhinus albimarginatus*, making off along the reef wall. As I swam around the point at 52 metres (170 feet) I nearly bumped into a 2.5-metre (8-foot) hammerhead that was swimming around in the opposite direction. We were both startled. The hammerhead reacted by throwing its head back and forth and snapping its jaws, before dashing off. It was gone before I had managed to take a picture – but at least I knew that there was one hammerhead around, and maybe more. I clanged my knife against my tank for a short while, in the hope of tempting it back for a second look, but it did not reappear. A couple of grey reef sharks arrived from the pinnacle above and came very close to look me over. I was surprised by their lack of timidity, but subsequently found out that another group of divers had started to feed them so that they were now almost tame.

The next day I decided to try diving off the south-west point again in search of hammerheads. As I prepared to dive I saw the grey reef sharks circling below, on the sand, expecting to be fed, and schooling barracuda just visible beyond them. Because I wanted to save my bottom time, I decided to snorkel out most of the way to the point, and then drop down from above. I knew that I must watch the current, however – it was sweeping off the point and could quickly carry me along the surface. I would have to begin my descent in good time, to avoid being swept beyond the reef, and the consequent indignity of having to be collected by boat. As the current carried me along, I could see the pale patches of sand on the point some 25 metres (82 feet) below. Past experience told me that a current flowing off the reef is good for hammerheads. I recognized a large coral head below and, setting my watch, began the descent to the coral promontory. As I approached from above, I looked for the sea whips: with their long, thin, flexible stalks, these can reveal both the direction and the strength of the current passing over the promontory. It was strong, and when I reached the coral I had to grab hold of a sea whip to maintain my position.

Barracuda *Sphyraena* spp. schools tend to mass on areas of a reef where there is the greatest activity. Perhaps the schooling behaviour is a protection against the numerous sharks beneath them.

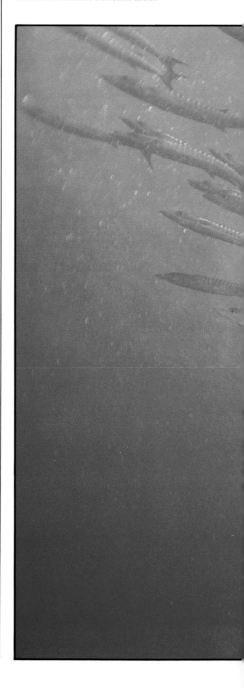

Left
A solitary scalloped hammerhead *Sphyrna lewini* moves along the underwater pinnacle of the south-west point. An occasional hammerhead is seen above the thermocline, but most are deeper.

Overleaf
A school of bigeye trevally *Caranx sexfasciatus*, a type of jack, demonstrates its reaction to what the fish take to be a predator. They charge an approaching diver and swarm at speed around him. A shark would find it all but impossible to single out one fish to attack under these circumstances.

As I swim out in search of hammerheads, the grey reef sharks, expecting to be fed, gather beyond the drop-off and wait to meet me.

The grey reef sharks had followed me out and were circling in front of me. I carried on down towards the end of the point and descended on the northern edge. At 50 metres (165 feet) I passed through the thermocline into the cooler depths and it grew darker. I gazed into the dim water ahead of me, but could not see any sharks.

I banged my knife against my tank but nothing appeared. I waited a few seconds and then started to swim around the point. Time was very precious – I wanted to be back in the shallows in five minutes time, to avoid the need for decompression. As I rounded the point, I was greeted by the full force of the current as it swept down the southern edge of the reef. I was tempted to move up the reef into shallower water, where the current was less fierce, but I resisted the temptation and dragged myself 20 metres along the southern edge.

Then I saw a pale flash out in the open water at the same level as me, and knew that there was a scalloped hammerhead out there. I started to hit my knife against my tank to see if I could bring it in. There was no question of my leaving the coral wall as the current was too strong and I would have been swept away. Fortunately, the hammerhead, a large one, responded to my clanging knife and moved into view. It was facing into the current, working to hold its position.

As I continued to clang my knife, the hammerhead, after a moment of indecision, began to swim towards me. It was a good 3 metres (10 feet) long. Then I saw another large one behind it, and another. I knew I must get beneath them; to photograph them horizontally in that gloom would have been a waste of time – I needed them silhouetted against the light from above. So I descended 3 metres (10 feet) further, until the sharks were outlined above and ahead of me. I could then see them much more clearly against the pale, distant surface. But they lost interest in me and began to slip back into the gloom. I started banging my knife again, as loud as I could, and slowly they reappeared from the underwater fog and approached. I took a picture but the strobe did not fire, despite having been checked just before I dived. Furiously I fiddled with it, and then resumed clanging my knife. To my delight six more large hammerheads came into view from behind the first three, widely spaced apart. Then I saw why. The big hammerheads were in a great circular formation, of which I had initially seen only a small part. As they approached I saw many more adults, forming a huge circle, and countless juveniles of less than 2 metres (6 feet 6 inches) in length massed together in a tight pack at the centre of the formation. The young hammerheads were, in effect, enclosed by a ring of adults. All I could see ahead of me were their strange shadowy, swaying heads. While the bulk of the school, eighty, perhaps a hundred strong, stayed away, a few moved over me for a brief inspection. I took a few shots. Then the hammerheads, large and small, retreated into the gloom again, as if they were never there. But I was elated. It was only the second day, and I had located a school. I now had a month in which to photograph them. As I ascended through the thermocline, to where the soft corals were dipping their tentacles into the food-rich current, I could see the silhouette of a reef shark overhead, still circling about . . .

After that, I dived the south-west point at the start of every day, looking for the nursery school. Once I saw them swarming over the reef below me as I descended. But when I got down, they were gone, and no amount of knife clanging would bring them back. The chance to photograph this extraordinary formation never came again – indeed, as far as I know, it has never been observed by anyone else, although scalloped hammerhead schools in which the different age groups are randomly mixed are not uncommon, according to Don Nelson. Why does the scalloped hammerhead school? The most obvious answer is that it is a defence against predation, and the formation of the Sanganeb school suggested just that – the young apparently shielded by a ring of adults. However, there are few obvious predators on the scalloped hammerhead. Perhaps a large tiger shark or a great white shark would take a small hammerhead but this is unlikely to be the whole explanation – the schooling seems to be out of proportion to the likelihood of predation. Furthermore, there are many other species of shark that are eaten by tiger sharks and white sharks, and they do not school as a defence. Nor do scalloped hammerheads always school – small ones are often encountered on their own.

Another possible explanation is that the schools are formed for reproductive purposes. However, this is unlikely as the majority of the members are mature females or juveniles – and the formation which I observed seems incompatible with such an explanation. In fact, all of the scalloped hammerheads that I have been able to sex in the Red Sea have been females. They are often covered in bite marks, presumably mating scars, although it has been suggested that females also bite each other to establish dominance within a school, or in competition for the few available males.

The three large scalloped hammerheads that first came into view beneath the thermocline. They are pointing into the current and must swim strongly just to maintain their position. At this stage I had no idea what was hidden in the gloom behind them.

Studying the schooling hammerheads at Sanganeb would be all but impossible: they tend to be very deep and rarely encountered. However, the schools in the Gulf of California are at shallower depths and often seen. This has allowed Don Nelson and his colleague, Peter Klimley, to note several behavioural patterns among members of a school. These include butting other hammerheads, head-shaking, jaw-opening, swimming in a corkscrew motion and doing a loop-the-loop.

Given these features, it is likely that school formation by scalloped hammerheads is a complex phenomenon. While sharks are part of a school, they do not seem to be interested in feeding – attempts to attract them to dead fish in the Gulf of California were unsuccessful.

Overleaf
Part of the huge school of scalloped hammerheads. Though the bulk of the school stayed away, a few came within photographic range. Note how, even at this depth of 50 metres (160 feet), in gloomy light, the sun has caught the flank of the leading shark and is reflected from it. This sudden flash out in the underwater half-light often reveals the presence of a hammerhead. It has been suggested that hammerheads tilt their bodies to catch the light and so signal to each other.

In the dozens of times that I took dead fish down at Sanganeb, I never once got a hammerhead to come in. Grey reef sharks often came in from some distance away – down-current, beyond the range of visibility. It seemed inconceivable that no hammerhead ever smelt the proffered fish.

Another curious feature of the hammerhead schools at Sanganeb is

Large adult scalloped hammerheads enclose a densely packed core of immature sharks off the south-west point of Sanganeb reef. This species is known to form schools in other parts of the world, but none has been recorded with a structure like this one.

their relationship to the current. On those occasions when I saw hammerheads in any numbers off the south-west point of Sanganeb, there tended to be a current flowing in an easterly direction off the end of the reef. The sharks could be seen out in the current, pointing into it and swimming vigorously just to maintain their position. This is strange in itself – they must have been expending a great deal of

As I swim back up the reef face and through the thermocline into warmer surface waters, I enter the familiar world of coral heads and soft corals. Above, I see the silhouette of a grey reef shark patrolling the drop-off.

energy simply to remain in one place over a long period of time. They could have easily moved out of the main force of the current and behind the shelter of the coral wall, had they so wished.

Tagging and tracking studies in the Gulf of California do not throw much light on this: they have shown that schooling hammerheads there do not appear to position themselves in response to changes in the current. However, those studies also showed that at dusk the schools disperse – possibly individually or in small groups – to feed during the night. The schools reform at dawn. This might apply also to Sanganeb – perhaps the reef is swarming with hammerheads foraging for food during the night? At dawn, in common with the Californian hammerheads, they might gather in a school at an appropriate location – the south-west point or the north point. Here, in large numbers, other social activities might take place, including mating perhaps. But where are the males? And why choose a place with such a strong current? Like many questions about shark biology, this one cannot be answered – yet.

CHAPTER FIVE

SHARKS
—OF THE—
OPEN SEA

Just as there are sharks that have become adapted to life on the coral reef, so there are other species that spend most of their time in the vast expanses of the mid-ocean. Some sharks, such as the tiger shark and the scalloped hammerhead, make migrations over considerable distances of open ocean, but these are not true oceanic species, as they are often found in shallow water also.

Truly oceanic sharks are rarely encountered by divers, unless they are specifically seeking them out, because the great majority of dives are made in relatively shallow water near the coast. Occasionally, when the bottom drops dramatically to deep water, one might glimpse a passing oceanic shark, a visitor from another world casting a steady eye over the unfamiliar coastal waters. But that is all.

What makes life so different in the open ocean? The answer is immediately apparent to anyone who ventures far from shore – there is simply nothing there. Most of the life of the ocean goes on around its shores, on the seabed, or in the uppermost surface waters where the plankton – tiny floating plants and animals – are found. The mid-ocean is largely an empty underwater desert. But, just as there are animals that thrive in deserts on land, so too in the marine deserts of the ocean. And among them are various species of shark. The relative emptiness of the open sea is punctuated by tiny areas of activity: a school of tuna hunting small fish, a pod of migrating whales, a million mating squid, massing on the ocean's surface under the moonlight. And tuned to these rare events are the oceanic sharks. The second half of my stay with Don Nelson, in the summer of 1986, was spent trying to photograph the oceanic blue shark *Prionace glauca* in the offshore waters of California. This elegant, graceful animal is not only one of the most common oceanic sharks, it is also one of the most abundant large animals on the planet. As is so often the case with sharks, there are reports of gigantic blues attaining 6 metres (20 feet) and more in the literature, though these figures seem highly unlikely. A 3-metre (10-foot) blue shark is large and most adults are nearer 2 metres (6 feet 6 inches). The blue shark is found in all the temperate and tropical oceans of the world. It prefers cool water, between 7°C and 16°C (45°F and 61°F), but is also found in the tropics, where it prefers to stay in deeper water where the temperature is lower.

The blue shark has several adaptations that allow it to thrive in

open water. The pectoral fins are very long, which allows the animal to swim slowly, conserving its energy, and yet not sink. It is capable of bursts of speed when necessary. Furthermore, it can feed on a wide variety of prey. The insides of the gills are finely meshed so that small animals taken in through the mouth, such as anchovies, shrimps and open-water crabs, cannot escape. But the blue shark will feed on many other things as well, including squid, and a wide variety of teleost fish.

Blue sharks can travel great distances, as tagging studies have shown. Sharks labelled on the western side of the Atlantic have subsequently been recovered off Spain, and some tagged off the Canary Islands have been found near Cuba. It is thought that such enormous distances are covered by swimming in the great oceanic currents that run across the Atlantic, namely the Gulf Stream eastwards and the North Equatorial Current westwards.

Blue shark populations are often sexually segregated. In the summer, nearly all the blues found off the central Californian coast are males, the females being in the the colder waters further north. Blue sharks are viviparous and there is an astounding range in the number of young a female can carry. As few as four have been recorded, but the record is a hundred and thirty five young in one female.

During my quest for the blue shark, Mike Braun worked with me again, acting as my bodyguard in the water: while I was busy photographing one shark, his job was to make sure that no others sneaked up on me from behind. Don explained that the blues could be dangerous – the last diver to work with him on the blues had been bitten by one.

The method of attracting the blues is simple: a wire cage containing mackerel is dangled in the water off the drifting boat. The action of the waves gradually breaks up the fish and sends a chum slick out to drift behind the boat.

On the first day of chumming for the blues, our first shark, a male blue of a little under 2 metres (6 feet 6 inches) in length, turned up at the boat within ten minutes of our starting. But he did not stay. A second and third shark came and went. Two hours had passed, when we saw another blue shark below the surface. The brilliant blue of his back flashed in different hues as he moved, changing his angle to the sun. At one moment he was a deep Pacific blue shading to a silver flank. Then, as he turned, the silver would expand and drown out the blue of his back in a metallic sheen. Then a green trace would glow from his sides before vanishing.

Mike and I entered the water to see three other male blues of up to 2 metres (6 feet 6 inches) in length, a little further off in the chum slick. Behind them, flicking nervously back and forth, was a small shortfin mako *Isurus oxyrinchus*.. It was a totally different kind of animal. As the blues moved in a lazy, stately slow-motion, it twitched and sped around, just beneath the surface, the silver gloss of its flanks gleaming with each turn. And yet, for all its speed, it seemed vulnerable, as if a scratch could kill it. Mike later described the head of the animal as looking as if it had been put in a pencil sharpener and twisted into a point. To me, the mako has the fragile grace of the cheetah – everything sacrificed for speed. The beauty of the blues dulled every time I glanced at the flashing shape of the mako.

Portrait of a blue shark in open water. This is a slender species with a long, pointed snout. Note the position of the first dorsal fin, some distance behind the long pectoral fins, and the 'stretched' appearance. This shark is accompanied by a small group of fish.

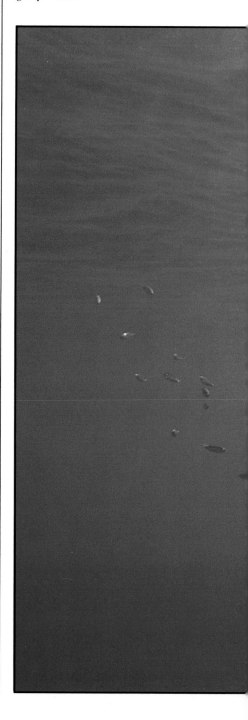

But the mako retreated into a silhouette while the blues, slow and fearless, moved in tightening circles around us. This increasing proximity was a little alarming. I was used to reef sharks, that might approach closely at speed, only to dart away. But these animals showed no inclination to retreat. They seemed to almost hover around us, so slowly did they move. I would wait until one was right up to me, take a picture, and then push it off. It would hardly react, turning away just a little, before coming towards me again. As the minutes ticked by, so the blues came closer and closer, and each time I repelled them they retreated a little less. They were becoming adept at sneaking up from behind. On several occasions, just as I was about to take a picture of a blue right in front of me, I would hear a

Overleaf
The shortfin mako is one of the fastest animals in the sea. It is a widespread and abundant species and sought after by game fishermen for its tremendous fighting qualities. There is at least one proven attack on a person by a shortfin mako and the species must be regarded as dangerous. The shortfin mako may attain 4 metres (13 feet) in length but most individuals are smaller. The one other species of mako, the longfin mako *I. paucus*, has longer pectoral fins, and a more slender build.

shout from Mike, and turning, see another blue behind me. It would not retreat, nor would the other, so I would thump them both on the snout. Still they would hardly react. I wondered as I gazed into their black, lifeless eyes, what plethora of sensory information they were gathering about me. It was obvious that sooner or later they would bite, if only out of curiosity.

By now a second, smaller mako had appeared. Like the first, it was swift and shy, keeping its distance. I very much wanted to photograph it, but this created a dilemma. The blues, large and slow, were now too close to be photographed. At this range their features would be distorted. But the makos were often too far away, although they were getting closer than before.

The situation with the blue sharks continued to deteriorate. Up until then we had been fending off one blue at a time, but now they were ganging up. I could see Mike kick his fin at the head of one and simultaneously elbow another that was looking under his armpit. Then he would spin around to push off one that was just behind him. By now, the one he had kicked would be even closer, and he would start the sequence again, while the third inspected his ear with sinister interest. I was having the same problems, and when one butted me in the back I knew that it was time to leave the water. Mike was happy to follow.

Back on board the boat, we discussed the behaviour of the blues. Don admitted that they had been unusually persistent, but then persistence is a typical feature of oceanic sharks. In the wide expanses of the ocean they come across prey comparatively rarely. When they do encounter something that might be edible, it is in their interest to investigate it boldly, rather than give it the opportunity to escape. Blues are not considered to be the most fearless of open water sharks, however, and unless there is chum in the water they usually do not approach divers at all.

A couple of days later we tried again. It was a beautiful day and the sea was much calmer than it had been previously. Again, we had to be patient, and a few hours passed before a large male blue shark came sniffing up the chum slick. I was already kitted up and, grabbing my camera, entered the water. I took up position a little below the surface and watched the stately shark swim overhead. I was surprised at what I saw. It dropped its long pectoral fins almost vertically downwards and swam over me, back and forth several times. I was at once reminded of the similar display by the male grey reef shark at Sanganeb. I knew that this blue shark was signalling something, as it continued its posture for a good fifteen seconds. Several species of shark, apart from the grey reef shark, are known to exhibit various threat displays. These include the Galapagos shark *Carcharhinus galapagensis*, the bonnethead *Sphyrna tiburo*, the scalloped hammerhead *Sphyrna lewini* and the silvertip *Carcharhinus albimarginatus*. Perhaps a display involving dropping of the pectoral fins is a widespread signal among sharks, which the grey reef shark happens to demonstrate at its most complex and spectacular level. I had never heard a report of a blue shark displaying, so, with some apprehension I photographed the animal. It then turned and set off down the chum slick. I saw that it was heading towards a much smaller blue shark that was keeping its distance. The larger shark proceeded to bully the smaller one – dashing at it several times until it retreated beyond the range of visibility – then returned to look me over again., Perhaps it decided that I was not to be so easily got rid of, as it ceased its display.

In fact ten wonderful minutes followed, in which this shark swam time and again into photogenic positions and allowed me to shoot it until I ran out of film. Another blue turned up, a little smaller than the first and with a deep and vicious bite wound around its mouth. This shark was also a male, and the deep puncture wounds of the bite looked to me like the work of a mako, rather than another blue shark.

Part of Don Nelson's research on sharks is concerned with the study of shark repellents. Given that sharks do attack people, it is obvious that effective safety measures should be available as protection for people in the water. This includes divers, swimmers and anyone who is a victim of a shipwreck. During the Second World War, sinking ships often forced hundreds of people into the ocean. Many were bleeding heavily and were the inevitable victims of shark attacks. An example was the troopship *Nova Scotia* which was torpedoed off South Africa in 1942. Of the 900 or so troops who were cast into the water, only 192 were rescued 60 hours later. It is thought that the majority of the others were killed by sharks. The survivors had ghastly tales to tell of the massacre.

Attempts have been made before to develop chemical repellents to deter sharks. The United States Navy produced what they call their 'Shark Chaser', a combination of dark dye (to camouflage the victim) and copper acetate (to chemically repel the shark). However, tests carried out over the years have shown it to be largely ineffective.

An exciting new direction for chemical repellency research was opened up through observations of a small, sluggish sole in the Red Sea by Dr Eugenie Clark, an eminent shark biologist. She wondered why the fish, called the Moses sole *Pardachirus marmoratus*, is so slow-moving that it can be caught by hand, yet lacks venomous spines or other obvious defences. Most creatures that are this sluggish rely on powerful armoury to deter predators. Dr Clark noted that Moses soles secrete a pale fluid and that sharks, under feeding conditions, refuse to eat them. On analysis, the secretion was found to contain a special protein which was named 'pardaxin'. This was shown to act on the sensitive membranes that cover the gills of fish, disrupting their normal capacity to regulate the water and salt content of the body. Laboratory tests showed that a large variety of sharks were repelled by the toxin. Unfortunately, it is chemically unstable and would be very costly to synthesize. However, the property that makes pardaxin so effective as a repellent is its ability to break up, or emulsify, oils – this it does to the fatty molecules in the gill membranes. Chemically speaking, this is not a difficult task – common industrial detergents have the same property, and scientists were soon testing a variety of detergents to see if they were effective in repelling sharks. One, sodium lauryl sulphate, was shown to be even more effective than pardaxin, and it is this detergent that Don Nelson has been working with recently. He mixes up a solution of the detergent and carries it in a pressurized tank on his back. Using a plastic tube connected to the tank by a hose, he pushes the tube into a circling shark's mouth and releases a measured quantity of the detergent into the mouth of the shark – from where it will be flushed over the gills. A shark that is to have the repellency test performed on

Overleaf
A mature male blue shark of about 2 metres (6 feet 6 inches) in length, drops its pectoral fins as it swims over me. I interpreted this as some kind of threat signal, although I have not heard of threat displays being recorded in this species.

it must first be tagged, so that if it flees after the test, and subsequently returns, it can be identified. Various concentrations of the detergent are tried on different sharks in an attempt to find the optimum concentration.

During the next two days that I spent with him, Don performed repellency experiments on the circling blue sharks. Their persistence in circling divers, which had alarmed me a couple of days before, was now put to good use – it made them ideal subjects for testing the repellent. Although open-water tests of sodium lauryl sulphate are in their infancy, Don was already beginning to get interesting results. A

Above and right
Don Nelson demonstrates the effectiveness of a solution of industrial detergent to repel a blue shark. The shark has been tagged next to the dorsal fin so that it can be identified should it return. The solution is squirted into the shark's mouth. It reacts violently, shaking its head and attempting to flush out its gills before fleeing. The fact that a shark attracted to a food source will leave the area and not return is a strong indication of the effectiveness of the repellent.

concentration of 10% of the detergent mixed with 90% water achieved a violent response from a shark. It would gape its mouth and gulp water, trying to flush out its gills, before fleeing, often not to return. (One such tagged shark was caught weeks later by fishermen, showing that the repellent had not killed it.) At 5% the blue sharks tended to take off, but less rapidly, and they often returned to the boat afterwards. At 2.5% the blue sharks would flush out their gills and hardly react at all. Don cautioned that the work was still in its early stages and that it was too soon to talk about making shark repellents widely available. What is clear, however, is that a common type of industrial detergent does repel sharks. The question that remains is whether a simple method of administering the detergent can be devised. Given the relatively high concentration of the detergent needed, and the fact that it must reach the gills of the shark, this is no easy problem to solve. It takes a lot of nerve to reach forward and push a tube into a shark's mouth, and for most people who find themselves face to face with a shark there will be little chance to practise.

The dominant oceanic shark of tropical seas is bulkier, stronger and altogether more aggressive than the blue shark. This is the oceanic whitetip *Carcharhinus longimanus*. Given the tremendous variety of sharks that thrive and compete in other habitats, this shark's oceanic dominance sets it apart. The oceanic whitetip is similar in form to the other sharks of its genus, yet different in kind. In the hope of photographing the oceanic whitetip, I joined Dan McSweeney in Hawaii, in November 1986. For the last twelve years he has patrolled Hawaii's offshore waters studying the remarkable variety of whales that inhabit them.

I had been pondering for some time how I was going to photograph the oceanic whitetip. It rarely comes close to the shore – indeed, longline fisheries have shown that this shark is more common the further you go from land. It is one of the most impressive of the requiem sharks, growing to over 3 metres (10 feet) in length. The first dorsal fin is large and rounded at its apex, the pectorals are broad and long – hence *longimanus* or 'long hands'. Cousteau calls this shark the 'lord of the long arms' in reference both to its pectoral fins and its stately form. The colour of the upper body varies in different parts of the world. In the Red Sea the back is brown, in the Indian Ocean, grey, and around Hawaii a pale beige. This yields, in messy splotches, to the white underbelly. The apex of the first dorsal fin, the lobes of the tail, and the upper tips of the pectoral fins are also edged in a dirty combination of dark and pale, that eventually yields to white. Sonny Gruber has suggested that these white fin markings are a species recognition signal.

The oceanic whitetip, like many other large carcharhinids, has triangular, serrated teeth in the upper jaw and similarly serrated, though more narrow, teeth in the lower jaw. These reveal its capacity to bite chunks out of large prey, rather than have to confine itself only to smaller prey. However there is one feature that sets it apart from other sharks, a feature that made Cousteau call the oceanic whitetip the most dangerous of all sharks. This is its astonishing boldness, its lack of hesitation when investigating possible prey. It just swims straight up and, as often as not, bumps the object under investigation. It is this boldness that has enabled the oceanic

The ancient sacred site of Pu'uhonua-o-Honaunau, on the island of Hawaii, is known as the Place of Refuge. The temple visible across the inlet is a modern reconstruction of the ancient temple in which the bones of Hawaiian kings were buried.

whitetip to prosper in the immense emptiness of tropical oceans. When an oceanic whitetip eventually comes across a potential meal, it does not deviate from its purpose. It was almost certainly this species that killed most of the shipwreck victims in tropical seas during the Second World War.

Yet these sharks seem to be able to use subtle, as well as stubborn, feeding methods. They have been observed swimming through schools of small tuna that were themselves feeding on sardines. The oceanic whitetips held their mouths wide open but did not appear to be attempting to bite anything. A few were later caught and dissected and shown to have tuna in their stomachs – presumably the tuna accidentally swam into their mouths in the confusion.

My reason for choosing Hawaii on my quest for the oceanic whitetip was that this magnificent shark comes relatively close to shore there – or so I had heard. The volcanic pinnacles of the Hawaiian Islands jut from the centre of the Pacific Ocean, and these waters are populated by an astounding variety of marine mammals. There are porpoises, dolphins, shortfin pilot whales, false killer whales, sperm and humpback whales, and many other species. It was the shortfin pilot whales *Globicephala macrorhynchus* that Dan and I began searching for in his small boat, because oceanic whitetips can often be found swimming with these whales. Find a large pod of pilot whales, and the chances are excellent that there will be a few oceanic whitetips with them. Why this is, nobody actually knows. Perhaps the sharks accompany the whales and feed with them on the squid that form the mainstay of the pilot whales' diet.

Hawaii's high volcanic skyline shelters the waters off its western side from the north-easterly trade winds. Thus several kilometres from shore the sea can be remarkably calm, making it possible to operate offshore in a small boat. Though we were a good 6 kilometres (4 miles) from shore, no waves were breaking – the sea was flat calm. We were following the 200-metre (660-foot) ledge of the island, for pilot whale pods are often encountered moving along the surface above this ledge. Dan has learned to recognize the different pods of pilot whales, that can number from twenty to sixty individuals. There are numerous differences, some subtle, others conspicuous, in the fin shapes and scars of the different whales. One pod is easily recognized by the bullet hole that has pierced the dorsal fin of a particular whale. Pods usually consist of many immature and female whales, that average less than 3 metres (10 feet) in length, and a few mature males, or bulls, that can be over 6 metres (20 feet) long.

Dan and I gazed across the flat water, looking for the glinting black dorsal fins of the whales breaking the surface. Dan was in radio contact with the sports fishing boats that were marlin fishing. The marlin had been extraordinarily abundant for the previous few days, and there were many fishing boats out. They reported back to us any whale sightings that they had made. The hours passed as we continued to speed across the ocean, searching for any disturbance on the surface. We checked a couple of buoys that were anchored in deep water. Oceanic whitetips had occasionally been found by these buoys, but there were none there now. Just then the radio crackled into life: 'Pilot whales spotted three-and-a-half miles off Kealakekua. . . .' We turned the boat around to head towards the sighting, and soon found the pod. It was a large one, perhaps fifty

whales travelling north. Dan explained that they were probably following squid far below, as sections of the pod would dive for several minutes before surfacing to be replaced by others. They were travelling quite quickly and I found it hard to imagine that oceanic whitetips could accompany such swift whales for extensive periods of time, for I had been told that they were rather sluggish, ponderous sharks. We drew up to the travelling whales and Dan began to photograph their dorsal fins, for later identification of the pods.

One of the large bulls came up to the boat and accompanied us for a short time, while the smaller whales kept their distance. A few had deep, raw circular wounds on them. These wounds, about the diameter of a golf ball, are caused by a curious shark known as the

Our search for pilot whales is relieved by this encounter with a small whale shark cruising slowly beneath the surface. Here it swims between Dan McSweeney and me. This individual, though smaller than the one I encountered in New Guinea, showed the same inquisitiveness before diving.

'cookie cutter' *Isistius brasiliensis*. This is a small shark that only reaches about 50 cm (20 inches) in length. It has a large mouth armed with very long vicious teeth. Its method of feeding is to swim up to larger animals, insert its teeth and, with a twist of its body, remove a plug of flesh, before escaping. Most of its victims are large teleost fish and whales, but presumably it could attack a diver just as easily. Luckily, the cookie cutter tends to stay deep down during the day, and Dan assured me that he had never seen one.

We stayed with the school for an hour, but they had no sharks with them, so on the next day we tried again. Dan told me that the fishermen were amazed at the number of marlin they were catching. Not only that, but the wind was coming from the north – the normal trade winds were disrupted. I wondered if the absence of whitetips

Finding travelling pilot whales is a combination of concentration and luck. This is the shortfin pilot whale, the tropical species. The longfin pilot whale is similar, but confined to colder seas. While the smaller members of the pod tend to keep their distance, the bulls are less timid. This large bull decided to accompany our boat for a little while.

could be linked to the odd weather and the unseasonably high number of marlin. That afternoon we spotted another pod of pilot whales, also travelling at speed, so I entered the water ahead of them and waited for them to come to me. Dan assured me that if there were whitetips in with them, they would swim right up and probably bump me. He explained that when they bump into him, he hits them as hard as he can and they usually move off. This suggested that when they are in with the pilot whales, they are less persistent and voracious than they are when on their own. Perhaps they feed well with the whales, and are not so hungry.

I watched the shadows of the whales as they approached, set my camera, and searched for the sinuous movements of a shark. But the whales dived beneath me and I was alone. A few second later, a

Overleaf
A bull pilot whale dives. Pilot whales can spread out over a considerable distance as they move along, driving squid beneath them. There is always one group of whales submerged while others swim on the surface, presumably catching their breath before they dive.

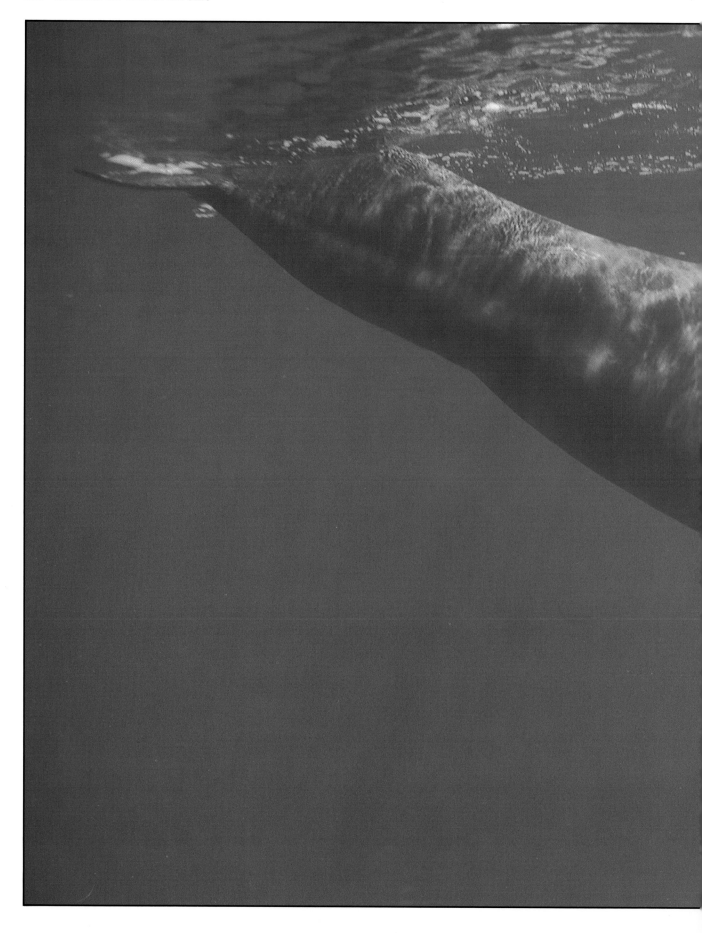

small Galapagos shark *Carcharhinus galapagensis* appeared, apparently trailing the whales.

Two more days of searching passed without finding any more pilot whales. The fishermen continued to catch many marlin, and the winds blew relentlessly from the north, making the sea choppy and unpleasant. On one occasion we spotted a few false killer whales *Pseudorca crassidens* that were racing along the surface and clearly hunting. These are tropical cousins of the killer whale *Orcinus orca* and are powerful predators. We followed two of the false killer whales, a mother and a calf, and they suddenly turned and raced towards the boat. Dan stopped the motor and we saw them speeding at us. Just in front of the mother was a large dolphinfish *Coryphaena hippurus* sprinting for its life. They passed directly beneath the boat, the false killer whales charging on. Then we saw that the dolphinfish had taken refuge under the boat's hull. We grabbed our cameras and entered the water to photograph this normally unapproachable fish. It was about 1.25 metres (4 feet) long, from the blunt head to the scimitar-shaped tail, and the colouration – dark browns and greens fading to yellow patches – identified it as a female. It stayed by the boat, exhausted and unwilling to leave this haven, while we photographed it. In the background we could hear the echo-locating squeaks of the false killer whales, but they kept their distance. Later, Dan told me that he had been in the water while false killer whales were actually eating captured dolphinfish. On one occasion, a killer whale swam up to him with a dolphinfish in its mouth, and released it in front of him, clearly offering him the fish!

Several more days passed without us finding the sharks, but at

Above
The female dolphinfish taking shelter under Dan McSweeney's boat to escape the false killer whales that were chasing it. Dolphinfish are instinctively attracted to floating objects on the surface, and will hunt for fish under mats of floating weed.

Right
This immature Galapagos shark was the first shark I saw shadowing the pilot whales. Galapagos sharks are among the most impressive of requiem sharks, with a maximum reported size of 3.7 metres (12 feet). They are normally found in the vicinity of oceanic islands.

A blue marlin *Makaira nigricans* swims beneath the surface in the offshore waters of Hawaii. These fast, powerful hunters can reach 4.5 metres (14 feet 6 inches) in length. It is thought that the mako is the only shark with the speed and power to take healthy marlin. The marlin uses its bill to stun the fish on which it feeds, as well as a defensive weapon against sharks.

length the weather changed. The north wind shifted back to the north-east and the offshore seas calmed down. Suddenly, the fishermen stopped catching marlin and returned empty-handed. We began searching again for the pilot whales and oceanic whitetips and before long we were successful – perhaps it was coincidence, but perhaps not. There are many things we do not understand about the ocean and its inhabitants.

Once the north wind had dropped, the sea was flat calm, and we

After an hour or more of steady swimming, the pilot whales will suddenly come to a halt and form tight groups on the surface. They will often 'spy hop', that is, lift their heads out of the water to look at you. It is when they are gathered on the surface, as shown here but from underneath, that accompanying sharks will often appear.

saw the sun glinting off the glossy black backs of pilot whales far away. When we reached them, they were calmly resting on the surface in a tight bunch. A few popped their heads out of the water to look at us, before slipping back below the surface. And, mixed in among them, were the smaller, pale shapes of oceanic whitetips moving just below the surface. Even as I was putting my gear on, a couple of the sharks swam up to the boat to investigate, before weaving their way back in among the resting whales.

The surface is so calm that we spotted the sun sparking off the backs of these pilot whales from far away. They are resting together and we can hear them panting as they breathe, sucking great volumes of air into their cavernous lungs. As we approached, we saw the pale, sinuous forms of oceanic whitetips moving among them.

As I swim towards the resting pilot whales, an oceanic whitetip shark wanders among them at the surface.

I entered the water and started to swim slowly towards the whales. Ahead I could see them basking at the surface, an oceanic whitetip moving among them. Then I saw another whitetip coming towards me from my left. It was just below the surface, a little larger than me, bulky and majestic. Swimming with it were several pilotfish *Naucrates ductor*. These striped jacks have adapted themselves to accompany oceanic animals such as sharks and turtles. It used to be thought that they led sharks to food (hence 'pilot' fish). This is doubtless untrue, but they probably feed on the crumbs dropped from the master's table, and they may well relieve the larger animal of parasites. Pilotfish also gain a certain amount of protection by staying close to a large animal.

The shark was about 2 metres (6 or 7 feet) off, and I expected it to come straight up to me, but it turned away. I saw then that the whales had dived, and sure enough the shark had set off after the whales. It

The sun burns jagged patterns on the back of an oceanic whitetip. Note the large, rounded dorsal fin and broad pectorals of the species. Just as the oceanic whitetip accompanies the pilot whales, so it in turn is joined by striped pilotfish. They will often dart ahead of the cruising shark and swim briefly around a diver before returning to their host. A few other open-water jacks can be seen swimming near the shark. They were also accompanying the pilot whales but, in general, did not associate with the oceanic whitetips.

was more interested in staying with them than investigating me. I now saw another whitetip swimming below me, after the whales.

I climbed back into the boat and we set off after the pilot whales again. We overtook the pod and Dan and I got into the water ahead of them. I could now see four different whitetips in among the much larger whales. Two were off to the side, and did not deviate in their swimming to come towards us. But we were directly ahead of the other two, and they swam straight up to us, bold and curious. They came so close that I expected to be bumped, but they did not actually touch us. The whales were passing on either side, and the sharks immediately broke off their scrutiny of us to keep up with the whales. I swam as fast as possible to try to stay level with the whales, but I was too slow. The oceanic whitetips, however, were gliding through the water and staying level with the whales. I could not even see their tails moving, and yet they were swimming faster than I could go flat out. So much for their supposed sluggishness!

Only when the whales came to rest again, did the sharks swim up to us to take a look. Even after several hours, the whitetips continued to approach us every time we got ahead of them. Other sharks tend to loose interest after a preliminary investigation, but these approached time and time again. One of the cameras I was using has a loud alarm that goes off if water gets inside it, and at one point this alarm sounded. Before I knew it, all four sharks were swimmimg swiftly around me, curious and excited. I got back into the boat promptly!

I could now recognize each individual shark. The largest, with the small pilotfish hovering in front of his nose, was a mature male, over 2 metres (6 feet 6 inches) in length. The other three were all females – slightly smaller, and slightly more rotund. One had four pilotfish in

Above
The beige and pale coloration of this oceanic whitetip is typical of Hawaiian individuals. Indian Ocean whitetips have grey bodies. Note the small remora attached to the shark between its pectoral fins. The shark passed very close by, in typical whitetip style.

Right
The oceanic whitetip looks insignificant next to the pilot whale that dives past it. Whatever the relationship between the whales and the sharks, the pilot whales show the sharks not the slightest attention.

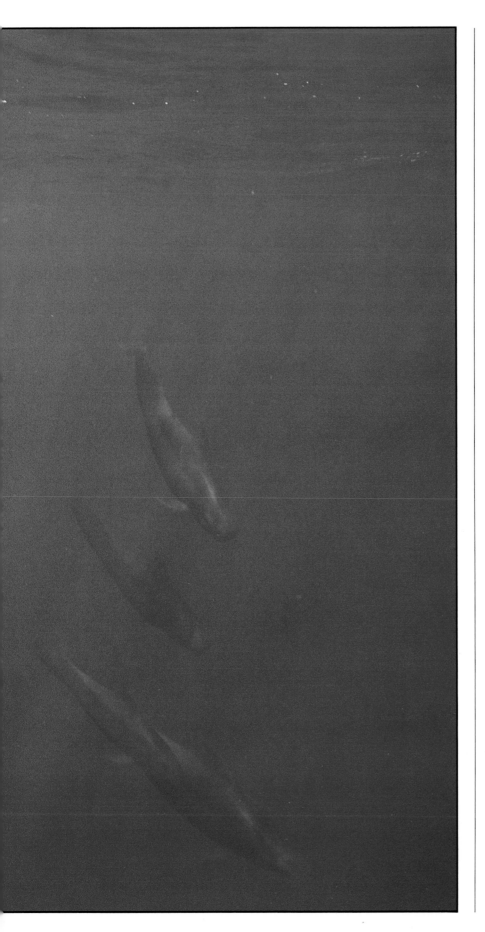

The oceanic whitetips continue to accompany the diving whales. The sharks usually dive down with the whales, but they occasionally follow from above. The most conspicuous feature of the sharks at this distance is the white coloration at the apex of the first dorsal fin. Given the boldness and broad diet of this shark, it would be of value if it could quickly identify other members of its own species, so that it did not immediately start hunting them.

attendance and two had none at all. When the whales stopped swimming and gathered together, the pilotfish tended to swim away from the milling sharks and wander around. But, as soon as the whales began to move, the pilotfish returned to their original sharks and accompanied them on their journey.

There was only one occasion on which I evoked a different kind of response from one of the whitetips. The whales were again travelling and Dan had dropped me in the water ahead of them. As I saw the dark bulky shapes of the approaching whales, I realized that the sharks were off to one side of me. Unless I got ahead of them, they would pass by and I would not get any pictures. So I swam rapidly to block off one of the approaching sharks. On this occasion, it was I who was approaching the shark — a reversal of the usual situation. Rather than swim towards me, as I expected, the shark tried to swim past. But I continued to swim in front of it. By now the whales had got ahead of us, and the shark was being left behind. It anxiously started to open and shut its mouth, while simultaneously shaking its head from side to side. Then it dropped its head and dived vertically downwards at high speed. There were a few scattered jacks below us and the shark proceeded to chase them. The situation was a little ludicrous because it was nowhere near them and had no chance of catching them. They dispersed and let it rush around, still opening and shutting its mouth. The shark had been ignoring these same fish for several hours — they too were travelling with the whales. It never caught them, and once past me, it relaxed and set off after the disappearing whales. Its distress at the possibility of becoming separated from the whale pod was evident, and added to my sense of wonder about these sharks and their unexplained association with the pilot whales. My final recollection of Hawaii is of the whales plunging and surfacing, with the oceanic whitetips accompanying them on their mysterious pact.

CHAPTER SIX

—THE—
GREAT WHITE
SHARK

No animal on the planet has been the subject of more hysteria than the great white shark *Carcharodon carcharias*. It is rightly feared, for its power and size are extraordinary, and it is considered by many to be the most dangerous of all sharks. Certainly, it has more attacks on humans *attributed* to it than any other shark, but one should be cautious about drawing conclusions from statistics of this sort. For one thing, most shark attacks occur in the tropics, yet great white sharks are uncommon there. Large, powerful requiem sharks, such as the bull shark, are abundant in tropical waters and probably account for most of these attacks, but it is often impossible to identify a requiem shark in these confused situations, so such 'crimes' are rarely pinned on a particular species. On the other hand, when a white shark is the attacker it is nearly always identified: size alone is often enough, though there are many other easily spotted characteristics – the huge head coming to a pointed snout and the black, lifeless eyes. The only other species of shark that are likely to be confused with the great white are other mackerel sharks, but none attains the gargantuan proportions of the great white. There is no doubt that the reputation of the white shark as a man-eater is exaggerated. It is certainly not the case that every great white shark which comes across a swimmer or diver in the water automatically launches an attack. There are cases where white sharks have swum up to investigate a diver and then departed. Don Nelson told me of just this happening to him in the Florida Keys. Nevertheless, it is obvious that a swimmer in an area where seals and sea lions occur could be attacked by a white shark out of mistaken identity, for these marine mammals are a major part of its diet. Such mistakes are particularly likely if the swimmer is wearing a black wet suit and fins.

The extraordinary thing about attacks on people by great white sharks is that most of the victims survive. Given the immense strength and large teeth of the species, it is obvious that a white shark could very quickly kill its victim if it so chose. But often the shark bites its human victims only once and then halts the attack. Perhaps the shark realizes that it has not bitten its usual prey, and so releases the victim. Another possibility is that this is normal behaviour for the shark – it may do it to conserve energy and protect its vulnerable eyes from the struggles of its prey. White sharks have been observed to circle someone they have just bitten, and they may be waiting for the victim to die, before moving in to feed.

Overleaf
An Australian sea lion *Neophoca cinerea* basks in the warmth of the summer sun on Dangerous Reef, off South Australia. The animals were once abundant on several islands but heavy hunting by man has reduced their numbers to less than 10,000. Great white sharks cruise the cool waters where the sea lions feed and seize any opportunity to attack adults and pups.

Whatever the reasons for these shark attacks, the fact remains that the number of people killed each year by great whites is very small. Off California, where white sharks are relatively common (though still few and far between), forty-one attacks were attributed to this species in the thirty-two years from 1950 to 1982. Only four were fatal – a death rate of one every eight years. Road accidents kill millions, yet there is no move to exterminate the car. The great white shark should be seen as an integral part of the marine ecosystem and not as a gothic monster, the legitimate prey of any sports fisherman who cares to tackle it. Though all shark populations are vulnerable to even limited fishing, the situation is particularly acute for this species. Growing, as the white shark does, to enormous size, it is comparatively rare: there is simply not enough food around to make it common. Combine this with the many years it must take to reach sexual maturity, and its low rate of reproduction, and one begins to see why each great white that is caught threatens the survival of the whole species. Many of the photographers and film-makers who have been lucky enough to study this animal have expressed the fear that they are merely recording it for posterity.

The great white shark is the largest predatory shark – only filter-feeding species such as the whale shark and basking shark grow larger. Just how big it gets is something of a mystery. Given the awe and fascination that this animal evokes, it is inevitable that there are wild stories of gigantic white sharks which bear little relation to reality. Some are doubtless due to genuine mistakes – for instance, accidentally identifying the superficially similar basking shark as a great white. Others are due to over-active imaginations.

There have also been genuine errors that have perpetuated the myths about gigantic white sharks. One concerns the jaws of a white shark from Port Fairy, Australia, caught over a hundred years ago and now in the British Museum. These jaws were described as having been from a white shark '36.5 feet' (11 metres) long. However in 1962 Perry Gilbert, a shark scientist, examined them and showed them to be the same size as the jaws from a shark that he had previously measured. That shark had been 16.5 feet (5 metres) long. So 36.5 feet was probably nothing more than a misprint – but it became enshrined as fact, and fuelled another great white shark myth.

The record is, nevertheless, impressive. In the summer of 1986, a male white shark of over 5 metres (17 feet) was caught off Montauk, Long Island. It weighed 1,565 kg (3,450 lb). White sharks are known to get larger still and there is reliable evidence for whites up to 6.4 metres (21 feet). The possibility remains that there are larger ones still: Dr John Randall of the Bishop Museum in Honolulu has suggested that there may be 8-metre (26-foot) white sharks roaming the ocean off South Australia. He bases his belief on the enormous size of bites in the carcasses of whales from those waters.

However large the modern-day white shark gets, it does not approach the size of an extinct prehistoric ancestor, *Carcharodon megalodon*. This huge shark is known from the fossils of its great triangular teeth, that bear many similarities to the teeth of the modern white shark. The teeth, which can be over 13 cm (5 inches) long, suggest an owner 12 or 13 metres (40 to 43 feet) in length! This goliath of a shark is now extinct, though it may have died out quite

As well as sea lions, the offshore islands of South Australia also support fur seal colonies. The Australian fur seal *Arctocephalus doriferus* is considerably less aggressive than its sea lion neighbour. This pup watched me take its picture without concern. The adults doze while the pups gather in groups to splash and frolic in the tide pools.

recently, in evolutionary terms. Some scientists suggest that it was alive 50,000 years ago.

Like its present-day counterpart, this giant shark probably took a wide range of prey – most large predators have to be catholic in their tastes in order to find enough food. The great white includes teleost fish, other shark species, birds and marine animals in its diet. Its powerful serrated teeth also allow it to take great chunks out of larger prey, such as whales; it is possible that it literally eats them alive. And white sharks will unhesitatingly attack dead members of their own species, a gruesome spectacle which has been recorded on film.

Although widespread from temperate seas to the tropics, great white sharks generally prefer cooler waters. Here they often gather off-shore from seal or sea lion colonies, and wherever there are healthy populations of these marine animals there are likely to be white sharks. Known areas include the south coast of Australia, the southern reaches of the African continent and central California, though there are numerous other suspected areas. In January 1985, I travelled to South Australia in the hope of photographing the great white shark. Carl Roessler, a well-known underwater photographer, has been organizing expeditions to photograph white sharks for several years, working with Rodney Fox who has himself survived a white shark attack and is the acknowledged expert on the behaviour of these animals.

We arrived at Port Lincoln, a fishing town on the coast of South Australia and loaded cases of photographic equipment into the *Nenad*, a sturdy prawn-fishing boat, about 18 metres (60 feet) long. We planned to sail the next day, for a seven-day trip. On the *Nenad's* upper deck stood two yellow-orange shark cages, designed and made by Rodney. Each had observation gaps through which a camera could be positioned. The gaps were surprisingly large. Indeed, a small shark could get his head through if he wanted. But Rodney reassured me that all the great whites which turn up are over 3 metres (10 feet) in length. The smaller ones might just be able to squeeze their heads in through the gaps, but they would not be able to open their mouths!

That afternoon, a local fisherman caught a great white shark, which he then displayed at the end of the jetty. Rodney and I went along to have a look. My first sight of a great white – and it was dead, strung up by its tail from a hoist on the end of the jetty. It was a male (like most great whites in this area) and the claspers jutted obscenely from its belly. The upper body was darkening in death to a dirty black and the white of the belly was bruised with pink welts. The shark must have been well over 3 metres (10 feet) long. Purple blood dribbled out of its smashed mouth into a puddle. Next to it, the fisherman beamed into a television camera, the hero of the hour.

One less great white shark. I tried to imagine what this shark would look like underwater, but, hanging from its tail, its shape was distorted: the guts had fallen into the chest giving it the appearance of a body-builder: huge chest and tiny waist. I moved out of the way so that the camera crew could get more shots of the grinning fisherman. After a few minutes we left, outwardly polite, secretly disgusted.

As we walked back along the jetty, I noticed an area of water, about the size of half a tennis court, that had been totally enclosed in a metal fence. I asked Rodney what it was, already suspecting the answer – a 'safe-swimming area'. The great white shark re-established itself in my imagination as something living, powerful and dangerous, rather than a battered carcass strung up by a fisherman. I looked out to sea, across Port Lincoln's harbour. Somewhere out there, moving through the cold, murky water, there was an occasional great white shark.

Early the next morning, our boat was fully loaded and ready to go. Already the horse flesh and tuna, that was to serve as our bait, had begun to smell. We had seven days to find a great white shark – or rather, it had seven days to find us. Two hours out from Port Lincoln, we dropped anchor off a small island called Hopkins Island. The blond sea lions that had been basking on the rocks came bounding into the water to greet us, and we photographed them cavorting through the shallows. But their presence was far from reassuring – they were the reason for the great white sharks being around. As soon as we had some pictures we left the water.

An hour-and-a-half later we reached Dangerous Reef, a small patch of rock covered in gulls and sea lions. It is called 'Dangerous' because it creates a hazard for ships, but to us the name had another connotation. We dropped anchor 100 metres (110 yards) from shore and the chum slick was started up: Rodney threw a cupful of blood and gore into the water. The exact constituents of his chum are a secret: if the fishermen knew them they would catch more sharks. I half-expected to see a great white shark in the first ten minutes, but I was disappointed. None came all day, nor the next. In fact, we waited for five long days before we saw even a hint of a great white shark. During that time, the trail of the chum slick constantly glossed the surface behind the boat. Every few minutes, day and night, another cupful of blood was thrown over. Rodney also tied dead tuna and horseflesh baits around the boat, attached to balloons that made them bob on the surface, so that if a shark arrived it would take the bait and signal its presence.

After two days the weather deteriorated and we had to leave Dangerous Reef. We took shelter in a mainland bay for a day, and then made a dash to some other islands, called the South Neptunes, which have large numbers of sea lions and fur seals – a magnet for great white sharks.

Sheltering between the two South Neptune islands with a vicious wind cutting into our faces, we could hear the din of the sea lions and fur seals on shore. Clouds of gulls swarmed above the surf, and the fur seal bulls displayed pompously to each other. The wind made us tired and irritable and the stench of the horseflesh did nothing to improve matters. Another long, uneventful day passed. Through the night the slick had been maintained, drifting out into the distance, carried by the currents and tides, pushed by the remorseless wind. But without results.

Then, as evening fell, Rodney suddenly noticed something. A shadow off the stern perhaps. Even he could not say what it was. He pulled in one of the ropes with a balloon and tuna attached – except that the tuna had gone. The rope that had held it had been cut through as if by a pair of scissors. 'That was a shark', he said simply. In these waters it is only great white sharks that are attracted to chum slicks or dead fish, so it went without saying that we had found the animal we sought. But it did not stay. We saw it once, a large, dark

Overleaf
Awkward and aggressive on land, sea lions become playful and flirtatious underwater. Here a group of mothers and their pups cavort before me. A bull looks on disapprovingly behind the bubbles that a pup is blowing.

torpedo-shape cruising beneath the surface. Then it vanished. Rodney explained that this was not unusual. A great white might put in a brief appearance, grab a piece of tuna and raise all expectations, only to vanish – perhaps for minutes, perhaps for hours, perhaps for good. It might circle, swimming in unseen patterns around the boat, or around the whole island. Great white sharks rarely hurry and they have to be coaxed to feed.

The next morning there was no sign of the shark. Only two and a half days left – we held a crisis meeting and decided to stay at the South Neptune Islands only until the afternoon, then return to Dangerous Reef in the evening if nothing more had happened.

But by the afternoon there was still no sign of action and our nerves were on edge. We decided to leave for Dangerous Reef immediately, so that the slick could be established there overnight. Even as we set off, we wondered if we had done the right thing. We reached Dangerous Reef in the late afternoon and immediately began to ladle chum over the side.

It was then that our luck seemed to change, and change dramatically. Only an hour later we saw a shark, grey-black, massive and excited, surging under the boat in the failing light. We watched him until darkness fell. Now we had the difficult task of keeping him there until the morning, when we could begin photography. The disappointment at South Neptune was still fresh in our minds. During the night he came and went, tempted to stay by the chum, which Rodney replenished every few minutes, and taking one or two of the baits. No-one on board slept much that night.

Early the next morning we launched the cages so as not to waste time. But there was no shark. Two miserable hours passed, while we waited on deck for a sign of some activity below. Then suddenly, at nine-fifteen, Carl shouted that the shark was back. In a long glide he swept below the surface, snatching a floating tuna before diving deep. We could see him silhouetted against patches of sand far below. Then he climbed back to the surface. For half-an-hour we photographed him from the boat as he surged back and forth, his grey dorsal fin cutting the air before he took a tuna, bursting through the surface with his broad and pointed head.

Things were going well – the shark was still there, and feeding. Rodney's instincts told him that the shark would stay around for some time. We got kitted up, trying to control our excitement, trying to concentrate on the photography. I was just positioning myself to enter the cage, laden with gear, weighed down by weights, when the skipper shouted that he had spotted another shark deeper down, but coming towards the boat. I half stumbled, half fell into the cage, and was shocked by the coldness of the water. Hundreds of small fish called 'tommy roughs' swarmed hungrily around the cage, picking edible fragments out of the chum slick. Carl was next to me, juggling cameras and grinning. I gazed to left and right but could not see a shark. I checked the controls of my camera yet again and waited. I looked to my left and dead ahead, Carl gazed to the right. Then I felt

My first clear view of a great white shark as it breaks through the surface, gnashing its teeth. In its excitement, as it moves through the chum slick, it turns completely upside-down.

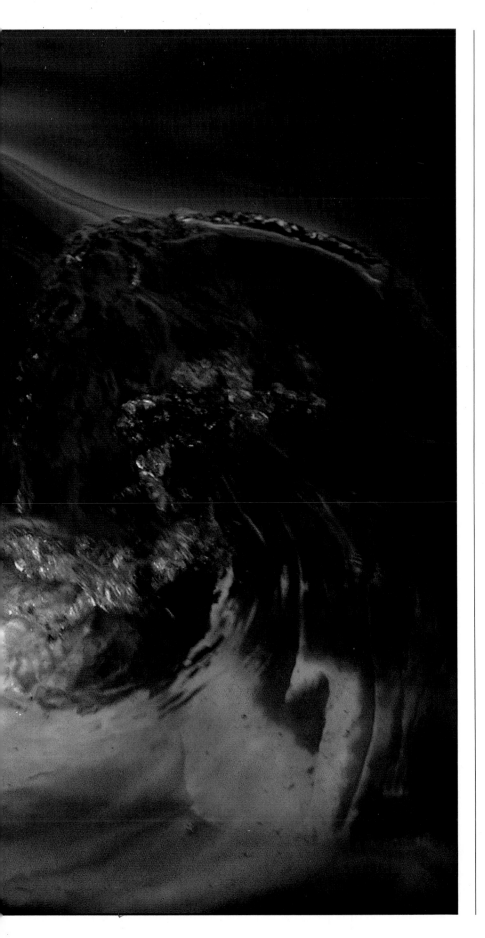

On another surge past the *Nenad*, the great white pauses on the surface to look me in the eye – an eerie experience.

Overleaf
Attracted in by the chum slick, a great white shark approaches the *Nenad*. The small fish that have been feeding in the chum scatter as it approaches the cage in which we wait.

him elbow me and turning, saw the shark in the distance, behind the small fish, fat and pale in the silence. Its bulk was stunning. From the surface you could not see the bulk – here, side on, I saw how massive the animal was, more like a submarine than a shark. The colour was pale grey with a brilliant white underside. It did not even seem to swim like a shark. The massive bulk of the body did not move, but was ominously still. Behind it, beating in isolation, was the crescent-shaped tail, grey and splotched with white. The shark must have been well over 4 metres (13 feet) in length and probably weighed over a ton.

The head was grotesque, scarred by the struggles of its victims. From the long gills forward to the point of the snout, the head seemed so complex in shape and contour, that at every angle it took on a different appearance. Head-on, there was only that extraordinary grin. The eyes, large, black and lifeless, did not seem to move in their sockets. They were matt black and unreflective, all-seeing and yet blind.

It was then that I realized how appropriately this shark has been named the *great* white shark, rather than just the white shark. Its scale seemed out of place in our modern, safe world. I remembered Rodney saying that every time he saw a white shark he was amazed anew by its girth, its length, though he must have seen more great whites than anyone else. 'When you see one from the cage, you'll ask yourself how anything can be that large, let alone a shark,' he had said, a couple of nights before. I realized now that he was right.

The first shark moved off, out of the range of visibility, but the other shark, a slightly smaller one, was coming to the bait. The bright

Left
Capable of unbridled ferocity, the great white shark is also a master of patience. Here, one swims by a suspended piece of horseflesh without taking it. The water is stained by the blood slick, and yet the shark is calm and cautious.

Above
The deep gouges and scars around the eye may well have been caused by the struggles of some hapless sea lion or fur seal. When the shark bites its prey, it rolls its eyes backwards in their sockets for protection. They then appear white as the sclera is exposed, the pupil being protected within the skull.

sunlight penetrated the upper water and he gleamed as he approached. I expected him to grab the horseflesh but he did not. Instead he glided past, investigating without reacting, his scarred, pointed snout cutting through the water. He moved in front of the cage, his pectoral fins sweeping past like wings, followed by the swollen belly and the beating tail. He came around again, in a long, curved arc, and headed for the bait. This time I was sure he would take it, but again he declined, angling his fins to swim just past the meat without feeding. Then he was gone.

Carl and I peered into the cold water stained by the chum slick. The tommy roughs swirled and gathered around us but the sharks had retreated. Then, far below, over the sand and the seaweed, I made out the black mass of one of them, swimming just over the bottom. A

This time the meat is taken deliberately, without hesitation. The food is engulfed in a lazy yawn as the shark exposes ranks of white triangular teeth. The thick nylon rope is severed effortlessly. A great white will open its mouth wider than seems necessary and long before it bites.

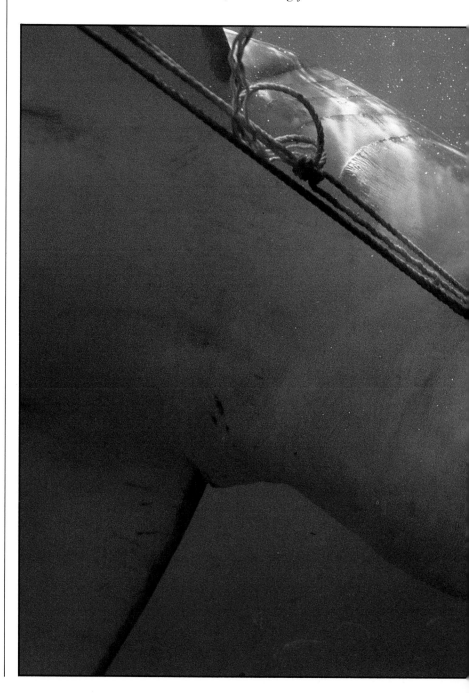

large ray was also down there, over 2 metres (6 feet 6 inches) wide. The shark followed the ray for a short distance but the ray did not seem overly concerned. It turned and the shark moved off. Then I felt a kick from Carl and, turning, saw the beating tail of the larger great white as he retreated. The tuna which we had put out as bait was gone. Carl shook his head in dismay – how had we both missed him coming in? I suspected that the shark had deliberately timed his approach so that he could sneak in from behind us. It made me wonder how many sea lions must, without warning, have found themselves crushed in those unforgiving jaws.

Again, we were alone in the ocean, gazing around us and peering down to the bottom. Minutes passed. Perhaps the sharks had gone for good. Then I saw one coming in from the side, straight for the new

Overleaf
Another great white swims by our cage just beneath the surface, the sun's rays illuminating its back. The shape of the caudal keel can be seen although the tail itself is not visible.

bait that Carl and I had positioned in front of our cage. This time
there was no hesitation. The shark engulfed the horseflesh with a lazy
yawn. As the mouth opened, so the teeth, in their white triangular
ranks, were revealed. The shark sliced through the thick nylon rope
that held the meat without even noticing it. As I was watching him
make off, the larger shark materialized out of the fog of chum dead
ahead. Again I suspected that he had sneaked in, this time hiding in
the chum slick – stealth allied with power. He gaped, butted at the
cage with his snout, then turned, the white bulk of his belly flashing
in the sun. For a moment he became wrapped in one of the ropes that
held the cage in position. He shrugged his body but the rope
constrained him. He twisted without any display of panic, and calmly
tried again to free himself. Again he was constrained. He turned a
little, and then surged off, suddenly free. As he made off, he grabbed
a tuna that was hanging a little further away. Meanwhile the smaller
shark was investigating the occupants of the other cage. I envied
them his close attention as they frantically took pictures.

Someone on the boat threw down another piece of tuna as bait. I
wanted to position it in front of our cage so I reached my arm out to
grab the rope that it was attached to. I felt safe enough, since both
sharks were off to the right. But even as I was trying to grab the rope,
I glanced to my left and saw a third shark heading straight for my
arm. I quickly withdrew and the shark cruised in front of me. Carl
had been engrossed in watching the other two sharks and I saw him
jump when this newcomer sailed in beside him. It was a male again,
about the size of the other, smaller shark – a little over 3 metres (10
feet) in length.

The sharks had stopped feeding and were now just circling. I
noticed that they always kept some distance apart from each other,
and then I saw why. At one point, the larger great white headed
towards one of the smaller ones, and the smaller shark panicked,
charging off at high speed. It was clearly terrified of the larger shark.

I was, by then, very cold and low on air, so I climbed back into the
Nenad. Carl also left the cage to warm up on deck so when I
re-entered I had the cage all to myself and could cover every angle.
But by then the sharks were just circling at long range, and although
I waited for several hours, and patiently tied pieces of horseflesh and
tuna next to the cage, they would not come close and feed. The light
was beginning to fail and I knew that the best hours for photography
had passed. Nevertheless, I waited and watched, enjoying the sight
of these unbelievable animals. Finally at dusk, when it was much too
dark to take pictures, the sharks started to feed again. One moment
they were circling and then they came in, one after another, to take
the offerings. Such are the frustrations of photographing sharks.

The next day was our last – a sunny, calm day perfect for our task.
And the sharks had stayed through the night and were cruising
patiently off the stern. Our luck had certainly changed! We kitted up
and entered the cages, again amazed by the size of these animals,
their grotesque majesty. There were several more sharks now. Four
cruising on the surface, and a couple deeper down. I recognized two
of the sharks from yesterday. The baits were in position and we
waited for the sharks to start to feed. For the first half-hour they paid
attention to the other cage and the food around it while Carl and I
waited in our cage with mounting irritation. Yet this gave us a chance

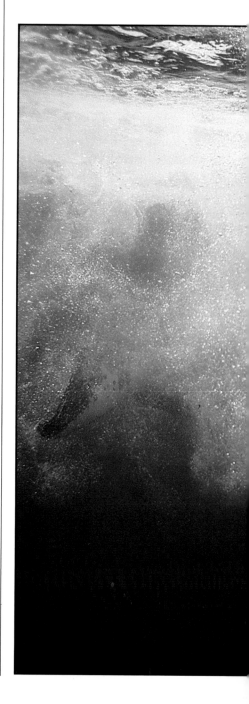

to observe the sharks about 12 metres (40 feet) below us on the sand. One was much larger than the others. Or rather, it was a little longer, but with the most incredible girth. It looked twice as broad in the body as the others. Compared to him, they appeared puny. And yet, when they came up to the surface and passed by, I saw how large they were. The giant stayed down deep, swimming back and forth on the edge of visibility. He would not come up to the surface.

The hours ticked by. For long stretches of time the sharks just circled, occasionally feeding for a few minutes. They seemed to have endless patience. I kept half an eye out for the larger shark below, but it stayed down.

At last this giant among giants appeared to change its mind, and came surging up from the bottom in a tremendous display of power.

A 4–metre (13–foot) great white, his belly already swollen with food, throws the water into a white cloud of foam as he charges the cage.

Appearances are deceptive. The shark's head is much too large for him to get more than just his snout through the bars. The sharks would often bump into or bite the cages. The electrical fields surrounding the metal bars probably confuse them when they come close, over-riding the weaker signals from the food suspended in the water.

Overleaf
A diver watches a great white surging in to grab the bait. On occasions, several sharks will feed simultaneously. Fearful of each other, they will approach in rapid succession, always keeping a distance from other great whites, and revealing just how dangerous feeding great whites can be.

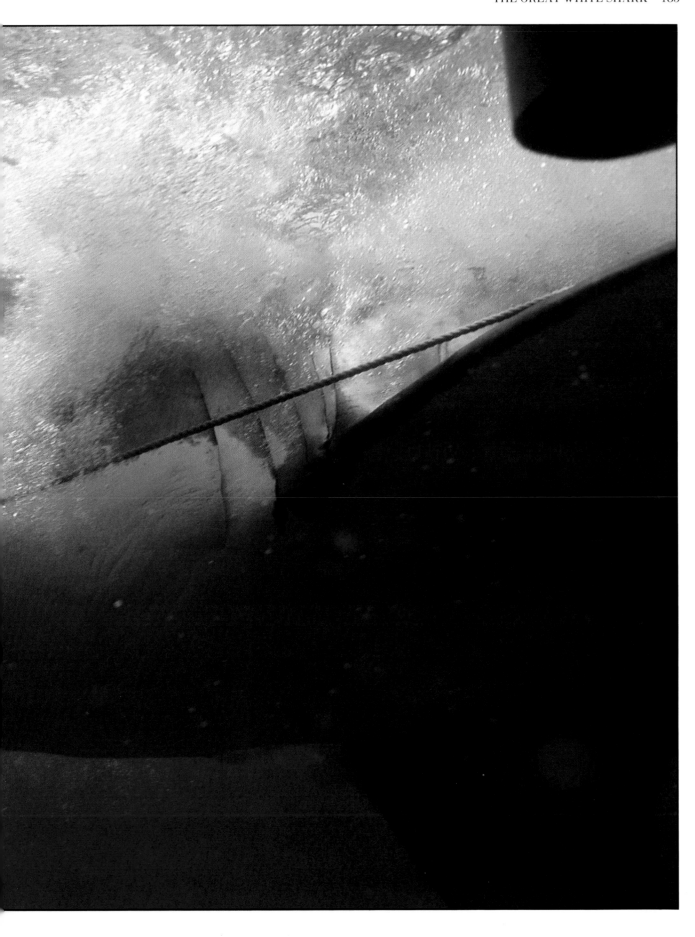

The other sharks scattered, suddenly seeming small beside it. It ignored the tiny tuna, the meagre chunks of horse flesh, as if these offerings were an insult. Nearly 5 metres (16 feet 6 inches) long, and twice as bulky as the other sharks, this one just came straight in between the cages and proceeded to bite the rudder, the propeller and the stern of the *Nenad* as if it were killing a bleeding whale. Then it started swimming down the side of the boat, biting as it went. In so doing it became wrapped in the ropes attached to the cages, and was briefly halted. Carl and I were thrown against each other as the shark lunged for freedom. But the ropes held, and he lay for a moment, vast and grey beside us. He seemed almost as broad as I am tall – nearly 2 metres (6 feet 6 inches) – and must have weighed well over 1360 kg (3,000 lb). Carl and I crouched there in a moment of unnatural

A feeding great white reveals a shark's ability to expose its teeth. The teeth of the upper and lower jaws meet each other as do the blades of a pair of scissors. The thick nylon rope offers no resistance to this awesome cutting power.

stillness, wondering what would happen next. The shark was trapped, wrapped in ropes. But we had not seen his full strength yet. He awakened from his trance, and with a bucking shudder, slammed his tail against the side of the cage to surge forward. The ropes tightened, and the shark lunged towards the surface. Then all we could see was the tail pistoning back and forth below the surface, driving the water into a froth. The rest of the shark was out of the water, held aloft by its massive strength, constrained by ropes. Seconds passed as he held himself aloft like a gigantic dolphin. The tail beat in a blur as he moved forward at a 45° angle, three-quarters of his body out of the water. Then something gave, and he slammed back down into the water free of the ropes. He vanished ahead in a grey surge.

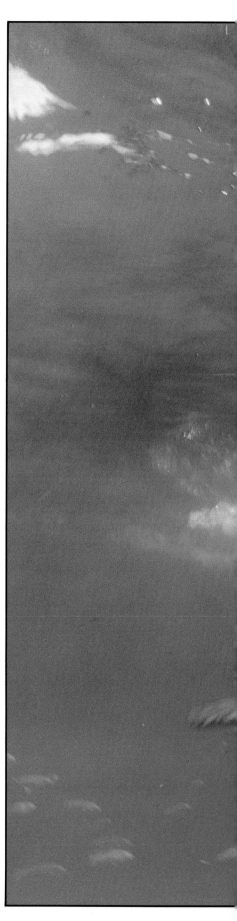

Top
The giant shark, the shark that attacked the boat and climbed into the air in its efforts to untangle itself, has gone. When it slammed down into the water it saturated the whole area with bubbles and it has taken twenty minutes for the visibility to improve. That shark has gone but the others have returned. Order has been re-established and Rodney has thrown a fresh tuna out beyond our cage. Already a shark is coming in and I start to photograph it as it gapes before the fish.

Above
I look through the viewfinder and see the shark as the shutter releases. I wonder why it has not taken the bait and yet it is still there, gaping and growing in size.

Gazing through my camera I cannot tell how far away the shark is, but realize that it must be coming for the cage.

Right
I realize I ought to retreat into the cage but even as I have the thought, the great mouth of the shark engulfs my field of view. There is a ramming impact as the upper jaw slams into the bars above my camera. I am catapulted across the cage and land in a heap at the other end. I look at my camera, terrified that the shark has hit it and flooded it. The camera is intact. I have the evidence inside to prove it.

For the next few hours we recorded the feeding of the other sharks. But it was a numb, automatic procedure. Everyone was stunned by what they had seen of this other, larger great white shark. One of the smaller sharks charged our cage, my camera almost vanishing inside his mouth as he butted the bars, throwing me to the floor. But it was the larger shark that I remembered with awe. When we had fed the sharks all the remaining tuna and horseflesh, we returned to the *Nenad*, exhilarated and exhausted.

Even as we were pulling in the anchor and preparing to return to Port Lincoln, a sport-fishing boat arrived at Dangerous Reef. The fisherman on board were hoping to catch a great white shark. . .

—APPENDIX—

A DIVER'S GUIDE TO SHARKS

To many people the idea of seeing a shark underwater is enough to quicken the pulse and bring on a feeling of dread. However, as snorkelling and scuba diving become popular, more and more people will encounter sharks, and this is for the good. Observation of these magnificent animals in their natural environment will help dispel many of the myths about sharks that have grown up in our minds.

The question arises: what do you do if you see a shark underwater? My answer would be: enjoy the experience because the shark is unlikely to be interested in you. However, it is worth noting how the shark is swimming. If it is moving slowly then it is going about its business and will probably soon be gone. On rare occasions, however, sharks will appear agitated or be moving at speed, and at such times it is better to leave the water. Such behaviour by sharks is more likely if there is speared fish in the water, and at dusk when they normally begin feeding. Grey reef sharks should not be followed, particularly if the animal becomes trapped against the reef wall and has nowhere to go but past you. No shark should ever be molested underwater; even the most docile bottom-dwelling sharks can bite if so bothered.

Divers are safer underwater than they are on the surface. However clumsy you may feel, once on the reef you are an additional part of the shark's environment: on the surface you are a splashing curiosity. On entering the water, it is better to slip in quietly, rather than jump in with a great splash. I have seen sharks react with great excitement, attracted to the commotion caused by a diver entering the water.

On the following pages I have listed some of the sharks a diver is most likely to see underwater. A few are easy to identify, a number are not. Many of the features needed to positively identify a shark are not obvious to a diver: for example, the presence or absence of a ridge on the back between the two dorsal fins, or the exact shape and number of the teeth. These precise anatomical features are often needed for requiem sharks and without them, little more than an educated guess may be possible.

The actual colour of a shark's body varies within a species in different parts of the world. In addition, its coloration is quite different out of water compared to underwater. Water absorbs different colours at different depths, and so the subtle shades and hues in a shark's body are soon lost. At depth, a shark, like everything else, will appear more or less grey. See the same animal on the surface, however, and it might be a breathtaking bronze, copper or gold, platinum even, or still just grey.

The stars alongside each shark's name give an indication of how dangerous each species is considered to be, with **** representing the most dangerous. Not surprisingly, large individuals within a species tend to be more dangerous than smaller ones because they usually feed on a broader range of prey, including in some instances, marine mammals. Fortunately, these larger sharks normally occur in deep water or offshore, areas where divers rarely venture.

Typical-looking, free-swimming sharks that appear grey or brown underwater; no conspicuous fin markings

▼**Bullshark** *Carcharhinus leucas* ★★★★
APPEARANCE Heavy body; broad first dorsal fin; short blunt head with small eyes; fins usually same colour as body although they can be dusky in smaller specimens. SIZE Grows to over 3.4 metres (11 feet). DISTRIBUTION A dangerous shallow-water shark from tropical and sub-tropical waters worldwide.

▼**Caribbean reef shark**
Carcharhinus perezi ★★★
APPEARANCE First dorsal fin higher than that of bull shark, very short trailing edge to second dorsal fin; short snout and comparatively large eye. SIZE Grows to over 3 metres (10 feet).

DISTRIBUTION A common reef shark of the Bahamas and Caribbean; also known from Florida reefs and the Antilles to Brazil. Large specimens can be dangerous.

▼**Dusky shark**
Carcharhinus obscurus ★★★★
APPEARANCE Difficult to identify underwater; relatively small first dorsal fin; second dorsal fin smaller than anal fin. SIZE

Reaches 3.5 metres (12 feet). DISTRIBUTION A large, dangerous shark of tropical and sub-tropical seas worldwide, found in inshore and offshore waters.

▼**Galapagos shark** *Carcharhinus galapagensis* ★★★★
APPEARANCE Beautifully proportioned with a long, streamlined body and high, pointed first dorsal fin; second dorsal fin about same size as anal fin. SIZE Probably grows to about 3.6 metres (12 feet). DISTRIBUTION Found off oceanic islands in tropical and sub-tropical seas worldwide.

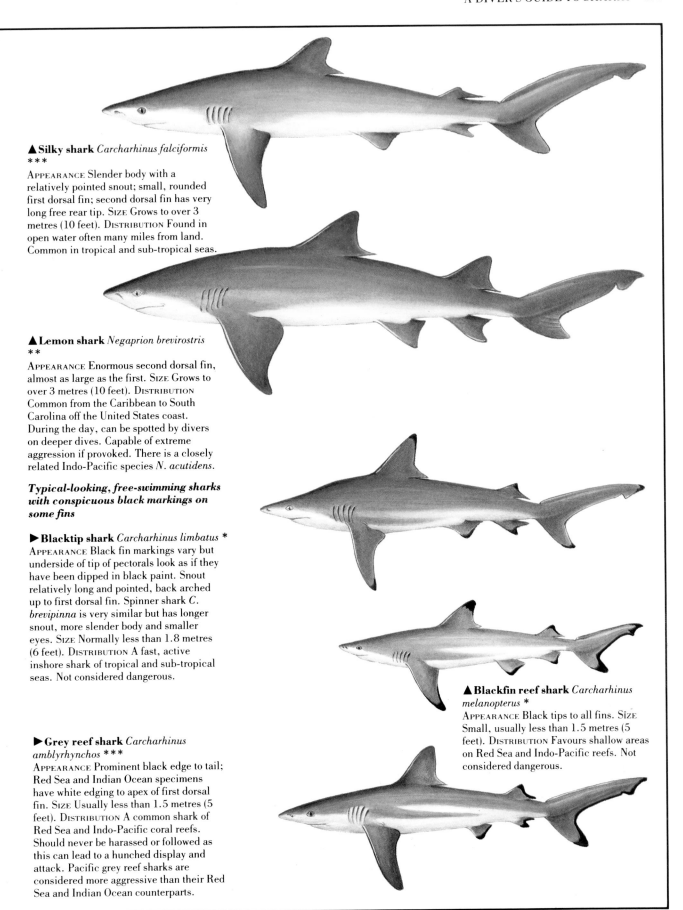

▲**Silky shark** *Carcharhinus falciformis*
***
APPEARANCE Slender body with a
relatively pointed snout; small, rounded
first dorsal fin; second dorsal fin has very
long free rear tip. SIZE Grows to over 3
metres (10 feet). DISTRIBUTION Found in
open water often many miles from land.
Common in tropical and sub-tropical seas.

▲**Lemon shark** *Negaprion brevirostris*
**
APPEARANCE Enormous second dorsal fin,
almost as large as the first. SIZE Grows to
over 3 metres (10 feet). DISTRIBUTION
Common from the Caribbean to South
Carolina off the United States coast.
During the day, can be spotted by divers
on deeper dives. Capable of extreme
aggression if provoked. There is a closely
related Indo-Pacific species *N. acutidens*.

***Typical-looking, free-swimming sharks
with conspicuous black markings on
some fins***

▶**Blacktip shark** *Carcharhinus limbatus* *
APPEARANCE Black fin markings vary but
underside of tip of pectorals look as if they
have been dipped in black paint. Snout
relatively long and pointed, back arched
up to first dorsal fin. Spinner shark *C.
brevipinna* is very similar but has longer
snout, more slender body and smaller
eyes. SIZE Normally less than 1.8 metres
(6 feet). DISTRIBUTION A fast, active
inshore shark of tropical and sub-tropical
seas. Not considered dangerous.

▲**Blackfin reef shark** *Carcharhinus
melanopterus* *
APPEARANCE Black tips to all fins. SIZE
Small, usually less than 1.5 metres (5
feet). DISTRIBUTION Favours shallow areas
on Red Sea and Indo-Pacific reefs. Not
considered dangerous.

▶**Grey reef shark** *Carcharhinus
amblyrhynchos* *******
APPEARANCE Prominent black edge to tail;
Red Sea and Indian Ocean specimens
have white edging to apex of first dorsal
fin. SIZE Usually less than 1.5 metres (5
feet). DISTRIBUTION A common shark of
Red Sea and Indo-Pacific coral reefs.
Should never be harassed or followed as
this can lead to a hunched display and
attack. Pacific grey reef sharks are
considered more aggressive than their Red
Sea and Indian Ocean counterparts.

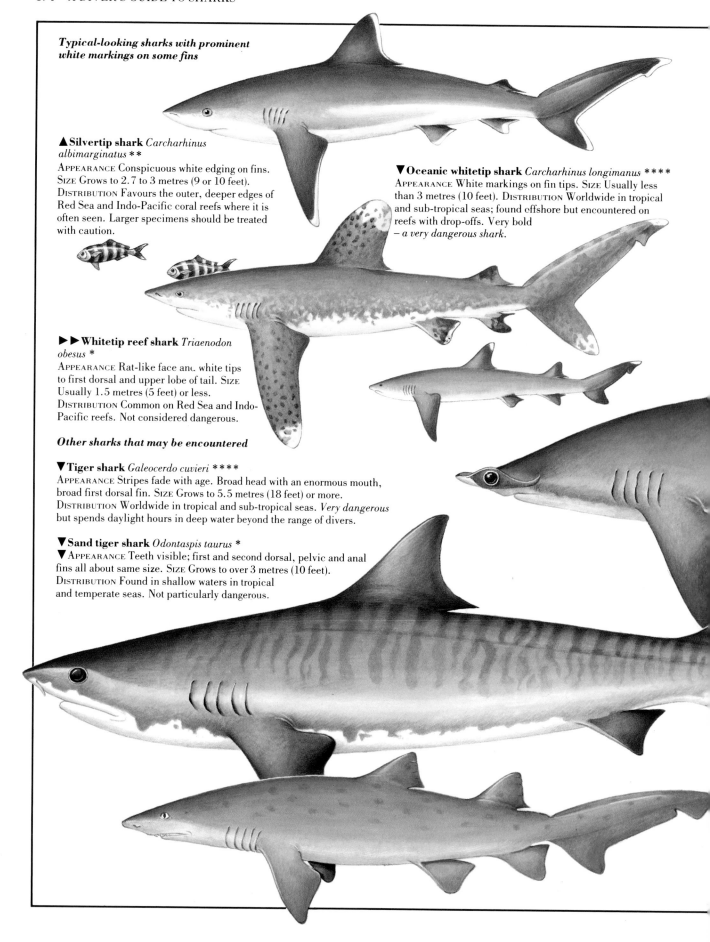

Typical-looking sharks with prominent white markings on some fins

▲**Silvertip shark** *Carcharhinus albimarginatus* **
APPEARANCE Conspicuous white edging on fins. SIZE Grows to 2.7 to 3 metres (9 or 10 feet). DISTRIBUTION Favours the outer, deeper edges of Red Sea and Indo-Pacific coral reefs where it is often seen. Larger specimens should be treated with caution.

▼**Oceanic whitetip shark** *Carcharhinus longimanus* ****
APPEARANCE White markings on fin tips. SIZE Usually less than 3 metres (10 feet). DISTRIBUTION Worldwide in tropical and sub-tropical seas; found offshore but encountered on reefs with drop-offs. Very bold
– *a very dangerous shark.*

►►**Whitetip reef shark** *Triaenodon obesus* *
APPEARANCE Rat-like face and white tips to first dorsal and upper lobe of tail. SIZE Usually 1.5 metres (5 feet) or less. DISTRIBUTION Common on Red Sea and Indo-Pacific reefs. Not considered dangerous.

Other sharks that may be encountered

▼**Tiger shark** *Galeocerdo cuvieri* ****
APPEARANCE Stripes fade with age. Broad head with an enormous mouth, broad first dorsal fin. SIZE Grows to 5.5 metres (18 feet) or more. DISTRIBUTION Worldwide in tropical and sub-tropical seas. *Very dangerous* but spends daylight hours in deep water beyond the range of divers.

▼**Sand tiger shark** *Odontaspis taurus* *
▼APPEARANCE Teeth visible; first and second dorsal, pelvic and anal fins all about same size. SIZE Grows to over 3 metres (10 feet). DISTRIBUTION Found in shallow waters in tropical and temperate seas. Not particularly dangerous.

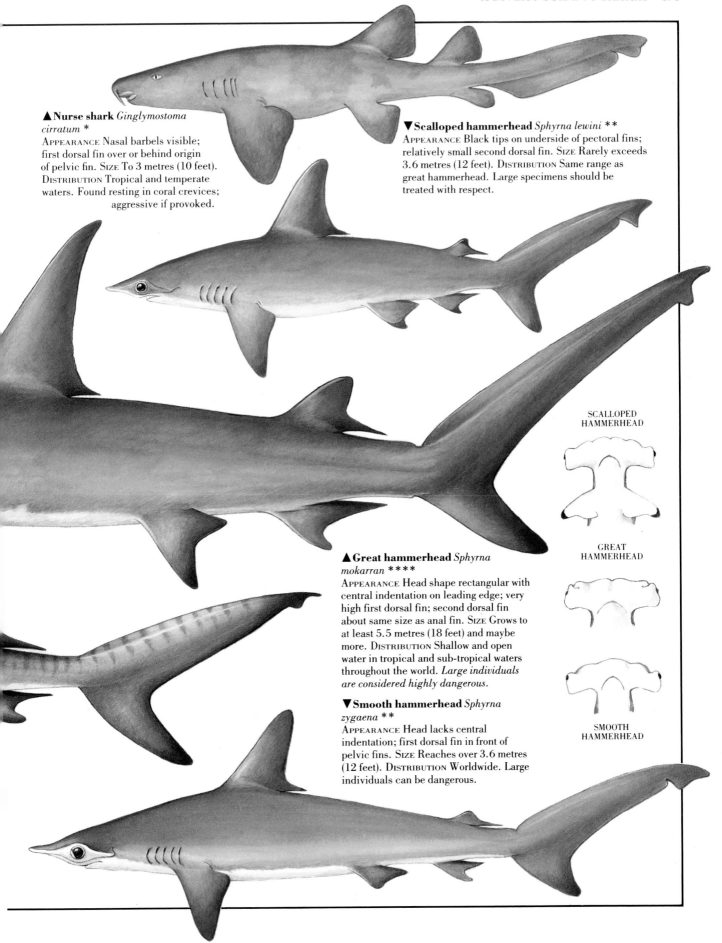

▲Nurse shark *Ginglymostoma cirratum* *
APPEARANCE Nasal barbels visible; first dorsal fin over or behind origin of pelvic fin. SIZE To 3 metres (10 feet). DISTRIBUTION Tropical and temperate waters. Found resting in coral crevices; aggressive if provoked.

▼Scalloped hammerhead *Sphyrna lewini* **
APPEARANCE Black tips on underside of pectoral fins; relatively small second dorsal fin. SIZE Rarely exceeds 3.6 metres (12 feet). DISTRIBUTION Same range as great hammerhead. Large specimens should be treated with respect.

SCALLOPED
HAMMERHEAD

GREAT
HAMMERHEAD

▲Great hammerhead *Sphyrna mokarran* ****
APPEARANCE Head shape rectangular with central indentation on leading edge; very high first dorsal fin; second dorsal fin about same size as anal fin. SIZE Grows to at least 5.5 metres (18 feet) and maybe more. DISTRIBUTION Shallow and open water in tropical and sub-tropical waters throughout the world. *Large individuals are considered highly dangerous.*

▼Smooth hammerhead *Sphyrna zygaena* **
APPEARANCE Head lacks central indentation; first dorsal fin in front of pelvic fins. SIZE Reaches over 3.6 metres (12 feet). DISTRIBUTION Worldwide. Large individuals can be dangerous.

SMOOTH
HAMMERHEAD

FURTHER READING

As I am not a scientist I have relied heavily on the work of others when discussing shark classification, distribution and biology. The works listed below are my references. They also serve as recommendations for further reading. Of these works, I should like to single out Compagno's Species Catalogue. This exhaustive work covers every known species of shark and is my main source of information.

Baldridge, H. David *Shark Attack*. Everest, London, 1976

Böhlke, James E. and Chaplin, Charles C.G. *Fishes of the Bahamas*. Livingston, Philadelphia, 1970

Castro, José I. *The Sharks of North American Waters*. A & M University Press, Texas, 1983

Cohen, Joel L. and Gruber, Samuel H. *Spectral Sensitivity and Purkinje Shift in the Retina of the Lemon Shark, Negaprion brevirostris (Poey)*. Vision Research, Vol 17, Pergamon Press, Oxford, 1976

Compagno, Leonard J.V. *FAO Species Catalogue*, Vol 4, Parts 1 and 2 *Sharks of the World*. Food and Agriculture Organisation, Rome, 1984

Cousteau, Jacques-Yves and Cousteau, Philippe *The Shark: Splendid Savage of the Sea*. Cassell, London, 1971

Ellis, Richard *The Book of Sharks*. Robert Hale, London, 1983

Garrick, J.A.F. *Sharks of the Genus Carcharhinus*. National Oceanic and Atmospheric Administration Technical Report, National Marine Fisheries Service, Circular 445, United States Department of Commerce, Seattle, 1982

Gruber, Samuel H. and Myrberg, Arthur A. *Approaches to the Study of the Behaviour of Sharks*. Amer. Zool.17, 1977

Gruber, Samuel H. and Zlotkin, Eliahu *Bioassay of Surfactants as Shark Repellents*. Naval Research Reviews, Vol XXXIV, Arlington, Va, 1982

Gruber, Samuel H., Hamasaki, D.H. and Bridges, C.D.B. *Cones in the Retina of the Lemon Shark (Negaprion brevirostris)*. Vision Research, Vol 3, Pergamon Press, Oxford, 1963

Gruber, S.H., Zlotkin E. and Nelson, D.R. *Shark Repellents: Behavioural Bioassays in Laboratory and Field*. Toxins, Drugs, and Pollutants in Marine Animals, Springer-Verlag, Berlin Heidelberg, 1984

Gruber, Samuel H. and Cohen, Joel L. *Visual System of the Elasmobranchs: State of the Art 1960–1975* from *Sensory Biology of Sharks, Skates and Rays*. Office of Naval Research, Arlington, Va, 1978

Klimley, A. Peter and Nelson, Donald R. *Diel movement patterns of the scalloped hammerhead shark (Sphyrna lewini) in relation to El Bajo Espiritu Santo: a refuging central-position social system*, Behavioural Ecology and Sociobiology. Springer-Verlag, Berlin Heidelberg, 1984

McKibben, James N. and Nelson, Donald R. *Patterns of movement and groupings of grey reef sharks, Carcharhinus amblyrhynchos, at Enewetak, Marshall Islands*. Bulletin of Marine Science, 1986

Moy-Thomas, J.A. *Palaeozoic Fishes*. 2nd Edition, Chapman and Hall, London, 1971

Nelson, Donald R., Johnson, Robert R., McKibben, James N. and Pittenger, Gregory G. *Agonistic attacks on divers and submersibles by grey reef sharks, Carcharhinus amblyrhynchos: antipredatory or competitive?* Bulletin of Marine Science, 1986

Nelson, Donald R. *Shark Attack and Repellency Research: An overview*. From *Shark Repellents from the Sea*. American Association for the Advancement of Science, Selected Symposium Westview Press, Colorado, 1983

Norman, J.R. *A History of Fishes*. 3rd Edition, Ernest Benn, London, 1975

Randall, Dr John E. *Sharks of Arabia*. Immel, London, 1986

Rowlands, Peter *The Underwater Photographer's Handbook*. Macdonald, London, 1983

Smith, J.L.B. *The Sea Fishes of Southern Africa*. 5th Edition, Central News Agency Ltd, Johannesburg, 1965

Steel, Rodney *Sharks of the World*. Blandford Press, Poole, 1985

Stonehouse, Bernard *Sea Mammals of the World*. Penguin, Harmondsworth, 1985

Tait, R.V. *Elements of Marine Ecology*. 3rd Edition, Butterworths, London, 1983

Wallett, Tim *Shark Attack in South African Waters and Treatment of Victims*. C. Struik, Cape Town, 1983

Watson, Lyall *Whales of the World*. Hutchinson, London, 1985

Wheeler, Alwyne *The World Encyclopedia of Fishes*. Macdonald, London, 1985

Young, J.Z. *The Life of Vertebrates*. 2nd Edition, Oxford University Press, Oxford, 1962

INDEX

(Page numbers in italic refer to picture captions)

ACKNOWLEDGEMENTS

I should like to thank all those people without whose help this book would not have been possible. In particular, I acknowledge the advice, expertise and help in the field received from Mike Braun, Bob Britcher, Rodney Fox, Jack Garrick, Bob Halstead, Jack Jackson, Giles Maynard, Dan McSweeney, Jack Randall, Mateo Ricov, Carl Roessler, Ron Schatman and Jeff Tatelman.

In particular, I should like to thank Samuel Gruber and Donald Nelson, without whose knowledge and help this book would have been greatly impoverished.

JEREMY STAFFORD-DEITSCH

EDDISON/SADD EDITIONS

Editorial Director Ian Jackson
Creative Director Nick Eddison
Editor Linda Gamlin
Proof Reader Louise Bostock
Designer Nigel Partridge
Illustrations Sean Milne
Indexer Michael Allaby